Property of the
Commonwealth of Pennsylvania
ESEA Title II 1972

EXPLORERS INTO AFRICA

By the same author:

For Young People

MEN WHO SERVED AFRICA

HE WENT WITH CAPTAIN COOK

THE HEBREW PEOPLE

A NEW LOOK AT THE OLD TESTAMENT

RETURN TO FREEDOM
(winner of the Isaac Siegel Memorial Juvenile Award for 1962)

MALARIA ROSS

THE STORY OF EMMELINE PANKHURST

THE STORY OF FANNY BURNEY

JOSEPH PAXTON AND THE CRYSTAL PALACE

OUT OF STEP

YOUNG MOTHER

NO STRANGERS HERE

Biography and History

HOW DIFFERENT FROM US:
a biography of Miss Buss and Miss Beale

HOPE DEFERRED:
Girls' Education in English History

RAPIERS AND BATTLEAXES:
The Women's Movement and its Aftermath

EXPLORERS INTO AFRICA

by

Josephine Kamm

CROWELL-COLLIER PRESS

12492 ESEA 172

Copyright © 1970 Josephine Kamm

All rights reserved. No part of this book may be reproduced
or transmitted in any form or by any means, electronic or
mechanical, including photocopying, recording or by any
information storage and retrieval system, without permission
in writing from the Publisher.

Library of Congress Catalog Card Number: 72–116440

The Macmillan Company
866 Third Avenue
New York, New York 10022

Collier-Macmillan Canada Ltd., Toronto, Ontario

Printed in Great Britain

First Printing

916
K

Contents

I	The First Travellers	9
II	Traders and Missionaries	16
III	James Bruce in Ethiopia	22
IV	Mungo Park and the Niger	41
V	The Niger Problem Solved	55
VI	Travels in North and West Africa	83
VII	Explorer-Missionaries in Southern and Eastern Africa	94
VIII	The Riddle of the Nile	109
IX	'How I Found Livingstone'	130
X	The Main Story Completed	140
	Table of Dates	152
	Suggestions for further reading	153
	Index	155

List of Illustrations

facing page

James Bruce (*National Portrait Gallery*)   36

Mungo Park (*National Portrait Gallery*)   36

John Lewis Burckhardt (*Trustees of the British Museum*)   37

Sir Joseph Banks (*Trustees of the British Museum*)   44

Captain Hugh Clapperton (*Scottish National Portrait Gallery*)   44

The Murchison Falls   45

Ripon Falls, Uganda, from a drawing by Captain Grant (*Radio Times Hulton Picture Library*)   64

Sir Richard Burton, by Lord Leighton (*National Portrait Gallery*)   65

David Livingstone (*National Portrait Gallery*)   80

Henry Morton Stanley, by Herkomer (*Bristol City Art Gallery*)   81

James Grant (*Radio Times Hulton Picture Library*)   112

John Hanning Speke (*Radio Times Hulton Picture Library*)   113

Emin Pasha (*Radio Times Hulton Picture Library*)   128

Samuel Baker (*Radio Times Hulton Picture Library*)   129

Florence Baker   129

MAPS

Explorers in Northern Africa   32

Explorers in Southern Africa   132

I

The First Travellers

STRANGE AS IT seems, much of the interior of Africa was unknown to Europeans until the middle of the nineteenth century. The reason lies chiefly in geography and climate. Africa has very few natural harbours and, with the exception of the great Gulf of Guinea, practically no gulfs or bays; and so the coast-line is anything but inviting. From north to south the continent is made up of a series of widely differing zones. The fertile Mediterranean zone gives way to the Sahara, nearly a thousand miles in breadth and one of the driest and hottest deserts in the world, scattered with infrequent oases and wells. The desert is backed by areas ranging from thick grass to impenetrable forest, and is cut by the valley of the River Nile, which rises in mountainous country close to the Equator. Few of Africa's rivers are navigable: like the Nile, they are impeded by cataracts, rapids or swamps, or they are blocked at their mouths by bars.

It is therefore exceedingly hard to reach the interior by river; and until the invention of mechanical transport it was almost as hard to get there by land. Travellers soon found that vast areas could only be covered on foot, since their pack-animals and cattle died from the bites of the tsetse fly and other disease-bearing insects. Countless men were killed by the relentless heat of the desert; many died from malaria and other fevers or fell prey to hostile native tribes. In the face of all these difficulties it is not surprising that for centuries Africa remained closed to the outside world.

The valley of the Nile was, of course, known to the ancient Egyptians; and the annual floods of the river enabled them to irrigate their fields. They probably knew the valley from the shores of the Mediterranean to what is now the city of Khartoum in the Sudan; but apart from the coastlands of the Red Sea and northern Ethiopia they knew very little about the rest of the continent.

The Egyptians, the first of the African explorers, were not the only ancient people to found civilised states in northern Africa. The Phoenicians, famous as navigators and traders, and the enterprising Carthaginians—also great traders—founded colonies. The Greeks were established in Egypt early in the sixth century B.C., and the historian Herodotus, who was in Egypt about 460, was convinced that the continent had been circumnavigated as early as 600 B.C. According to his report, Pharaoh Necho of Egypt despatched an expedition under experienced Phoenician navigators to find out if the southernmost extremity of Africa was surrounded by sea, 'bidding them sail and come back through the Pillars of Hercules [the Straits of Gibraltar] to the Northern Sea [the Mediterranean] and so to Egypt.' Setting sail on the Red Sea, the expedition reappeared in Egypt in the third year of the voyage. Each autumn they put in at some convenient spot on the coast, sowed grain, and waited for the crop to ripen before harvesting it and putting to sea again.

The Carthaginians must have made a number of expeditions but details of only one appear to have survived. According to a Greek version of the story, in about the year 470 B.C., Hanno, a Carthaginian admiral, was sent by the Senate of Carthage to found colonies on the west coast. Hanno, who commanded a large fleet, founded at least one settlement; he pushed on to round Cape Verde and, in all probability, to reach Sierra Leone. On the Senegal River he encountered 'savage men' and women with 'bodies all over hairie'. The wild men flung stones at the invaders; but Hanno's men 'tooke three of the women, which did nothing but bite and scratch those that led them, and would not follow them. Therefore they killed them and fled [flayed] them, and brought their skins to Carthage'. No one knows for certain whether these savage creatures were gorillas or belonged to some primitive human tribe. Opinion is also divided on the exact nature of the 'fierie Rivers' noted by the expedition and the great blaze of fires 'kindled on every side', but it seems likely that these were bush-burning fires lit by native people.

Hanno's expedition returned to Carthage because they could not replenish their provisions. It was not until the middle of the 15th century that a European expedition was to pass Sierra Leone, his farthest south.

During the second century B.C. Carthage was overthrown by Rome. The name 'Africa', originally given by the Romans to the country in the immediate neighbourhood of Carthage in North Africa, was later extended as geographical knowledge of the continent increased. Both Greek and Roman writers, however, referred to the continent as a whole as 'Libya'.

The Romans, who discovered a new route to the borders of Ethiopia, sent an expedition to explore the sources of the Nile. Ever since the days of the Pharaohs historians and geographers had been fascinated by the mystery of the source of a river which, until the discovery of the New World, was the longest river known to man. There were rumours that the river rose from some fountains deep in the heart of Africa but no one knew for certain. About 460 B.C. Herodotus followed the course of the river as far as the first cataract at Aswan* but could discover nothing definite about its source. He had heard rumours, he said, of a mighty river, swarming with crocodiles, far away to the south-west of Egypt. This river in due course proved to be the Niger; but, like many geographers before and after his time, Herodotus imagined that it must be the upper course of the Nile. He thought the Nile must rise somewhere south of the Atlas Mountains and that it took a long eastward course before turning north to flow through Egypt to the Mediterranean. He also had an explanation for the Nile floods. He thought they must be caused by the reduced evaporation during

* The first Aswan Dam was built in 1902 to control the Nile floods in Egypt.

the winter months which allowed more water to flow down the river. Argument went on about the cause of the floods until it was discovered that they were brought down, not by the main Nile stream, but by the Blue Nile as a result of the rains in Ethiopia.

The Roman expedition was sent out by the Emperor Nero into Nubia (the Sudan), with orders to trace the Nile to its source. According to Seneca, who had been Nero's tutor, after a lengthy journey the expedition came to an area of marshland, thick with mud and so entangled with vegetation that it was impossible to pass. The men also saw two rocks from which a river fell with tremendous force. Some doubt exists about the exact locality of the rocks: but there is no doubt that the expedition had reached the marshes of the Sudd region; and, although it failed in its main purpose, it had arrived at a point which was not reached again by Europeans for nearly eighteen hundred years.

A story about the Nile region circulated in the first century A.D. concerned the travels of a Greek trader called Diogenes, who claimed to have journeyed inland from the east coast of Africa and to have seen snow-capped mountains in the vicinity of two great lakes. In this story, as told by the geographer Marinus of Tyre, the lakes, watered by the mountain snows, were said to be the sources of the Nile. Both Marinus and the great astronomer-geographer Ptolemy were right in thinking of lake sources for the Nile, but wrong in thinking that the lakes were fed by mountain snows. Ptolemy's famous map of the known world (A.D. 150) showed the Nile rising from two circular lakes in the heart of Africa, the lakes being fed from a range of mountains called the Mountains of the Moon.

Ptolemy's map also showed another great river—the 'Nigir'— to the west of the Nile and flowing in a westward direction. His knowledge of Africa, though necessarily incomplete, was invaluable to later geographers and remained a subject of debate for centuries.

Throughout the classical period northern Africa was part of

the Mediterranean world, cut off from the rest of the continent. Its whole length was subject to Roman influence; but this did not extend southward into the desert regions where nomads and oasis dwellers had made their homes and adapted themselves to their harsh surroundings. There was no overriding reason why the Romans should seek to penetrate farther south. Indeed, since the southern frontiers of their provinces were not protected by natural barriers they were driven to erect frontier posts and settlements to guard against the threat of attack by marauding desert tribes. And so, as far as the exploration of Africa was concerned, a curtain descended which was not lifted until the Middle Ages.

In the meantime tremendous changes had taken place in northern Africa. Muhammad had founded the new religion of Islam; and during the seventh century his Arab followers invaded and conquered Egypt and penetrated deep into the country to the west under the banner of their faith. Deserts did not deter them. They crossed the Sahara to propagate their religion in the heart of Africa; and they occupied the east coast as far south as the island of Zanzibar, laying the foundations of an Arab empire.

Trade as well as religion was spread by the Arabs. Several caravan routes across the desert converged on Timbuktu, the trading centre near the River Niger in the western Sudan; and valuable goods, including slaves and gold, were brought to Timbuktu to be sold in the market.

The Arabs were famous for their learning and for their interest in geography and travel. It is possible that during the twelfth and thirteenth centuries they reached the lake area of Central Africa. There is a story that one expedition was sent to find the source of the Nile and actually saw the Mountains of the Moon and the lake from which the river emerged. But, since Arab maps were largely based on Ptolemy's and his works had been translated into Arabic, it may be that if the expedition took place it simply repeated the journey which, according to Marinus, had been made by the Greek trader Diogenes. It is

13

certainly true, however, that the Muslim practice of pilgrimage
to the holy city of Mecca encouraged travel and a knowledge of
other peoples among the Arabs. During the fourteenth century
a pilgrimage made by the king of Mali in the western Sudan
attracted a great deal of attention; and his route was marked on
the Catalan maps of the period.

The most celebrated Arab traveller was Ibn Battuta, who
was born in Tangier and set out on a series of journeys in about
1324 at the age of twenty-two. His object was to visit all the
Muslim countries in the world; and in the course of his travels
he not only visited Egypt, Palestine and Mecca, but reached
such far-away places as Russia, China and India. He also made
an expedition along the east coast of Africa, landing at various
points and getting as far as Kilwa in what is now Tanzania. In
1351 he started from Fez in Morocco and crossed the Sahara to
Timbuktu; but, like so many others, he wrongly identified the
Niger with the Nile.

Ibn Battuta was not greatly impressed by Timbuktu; but
two centuries later another Muslim traveller, known as Leo
Africanus, who travelled widely in western Africa, described
it as an important trading centre and a city of great wealth.
'The rich king of Tombuto,' wrote Leo Africanus in his book
The History and Description of Africa, 'hath many plates and
scepters of gold, some whereof weigh 1,300 poundes; and he
keepes a magnificent and well furnished court. . . . He hath
alwaies three thousand hoursemen, and a great number of foot-
men that shoot poysoned arrowes, attending upon him. They
have often skirmishes with those that refuse to pay tribute, and
so many as they take, they sell unto the merchants of Tombuto.'
Doctors, priests, judges and scholars lived at the king's expense.
Merchandise from Europe was sold in the shops: 'And hither
are brought divers manuscripts or written bookes . . . which are
sold for more money than any other merchandize.' The king
lived in 'a princely palace' and there was 'a most stately temple
to be seene'; but the people lived in thatched houses; 'and their
town is much in danger of fire. . . .'

This account of the importance of Timbuktu gave rise to all sorts of rumours and exaggerations; and travellers who knew nothing of the interior of Africa were ready to risk death in order to find a city so wealthy that its houses were said to be roofed not with thatch but with gold. Before this happened, however, a new era of African exploration had begun.

II

Traders and Missionaries

DURING THE FIFTEENTH century European ships began to visit the coasts of Africa in search of new trading routes. Trade between Europe and the Arab countries at the eastern end of the Mediterranean had already been established; many of the goods which Europe needed, such as spices, silks and fine cottons, were brought overland from India to Mediterranean ports to be shipped to their destination. There was an alternative sea route by way of the Red Sea to the Isthmus of Suez; but goods had to be unloaded at Suez and carried to the ports. It was a costly business, and the cost was increased by the monopoly held in the Eastern trade by the rulers of Egypt, who exacted a toll before the goods reached their markets.

The first Europeans to arrive on the scene were the Portuguese. They were anxious to promote their sea trade. They were also anxious to break the Egyptian monopoly and to transport goods in their own ships instead of in the ships of the rich merchants of Venice who were in league with Egypt and had been given the right to distribute the goods which were brought to Europe by the Red Sea route. They did not think that trade with Africa would ever be important; and so for the most part they kept to the coast, buying from the West African coastal tribes small quantities of such goods as ivory, gold-dust and pepper. They believed, however, that it might be possible to sail round Africa to India and so establish trade with India direct.

The first stage in the search for a sea route was an exploration of the west African coasts. This task owed much to the inspiration and encouragement of Prince Henry, known as 'the Navigator', son of the King of Portugal and a grandson of

England's John of Gaunt. Prince Henry, who did not sail with the expeditions, was eager to further exploration and, at the same time, to extend Portugal's empire and trade. Improvements had gradually been made in ship-building and in the science of navigation and geography; yet, despite earlier voyages, knowledge of the west coast did not extend beyond Cape Bojador on the Rio de Oro. By 1445 Prince Henry's ships had reached Cape Verde and the Senegal River. By 1462, two years after his death, they had arrived in the Gulf of Guinea.

Expeditions continued along the coast. In 1484 Diego Cam discovered the mouth of the River Congo; and in the course of his voyages he discovered more than 1,400 miles of coastline. Then came Bartholomew Dias who, leaving Portugal in 1487, started his real exploration where Cam had left it—in the estuary of the Congo; and went on to survey the coast as far south as Walvis Bay in South West Africa. Sailing on, he rounded the Cape of Good Hope and followed the coast eastward as far as the Great Fish River. He arrived back in Lisbon at the end of 1488, having added a further 1,260 miles to Cam's total.

The adventurous navigator Vasco da Gama was entrusted with the task of completing the discovery of a sea route to India. Christopher Columbus, sailing for India from Spain, had struck bravely westward across the open sea to arrive, instead, in the West Indies and the continent of America. Da Gama struck out with equal courage from the Cape Verde islands and sailed southward in a wide arc until, some three months later, he saw land at St Helena Bay in the south. He then rounded the Cape, sailed up the coast of Natal and Mozambique as far as Malindi in Kenya where he took on an Arab pilot. Then, striking boldly across the open sea again, on May 16th, 1498, his ships cast anchor off Calicut (Kozhikode) on the coast of Kerala, in south-west India.

With the success of da Gama's voyage the Portuguese gained their objective. They had opened up a new route to India and the East; and, in so doing, they had set up a number of trading posts along the west coast of Africa. In the years which followed they established additional trading posts: but, as the power of Portugal began to wane, other European nations were hopeful of usurping her position. English, Dutch and French sailors visited the west coast to trade with the coastal tribes. Before very long this small trade gave way to a large and infinitely more profitable trade—the slave trade. When western nations founded colonies overseas they imported slaves for labour in mines and plantations. The supply of slaves seemed endless, for chiefs in the interior of Africa warred against one another with the sole purpose of sending their prisoners to the coast and selling them to the visiting traders. The traders had no wish to form colonies on the west coast of Africa, for the climate was unhealthy and the interior scarcely known. Instead, they built a chain of strongly fortified trading-posts, in which the slaves were collected and housed before the voyage across the Atlantic to the New World. Before very long this dreadful trade had reached vast proportions. In the meantime, the exploration of the outline of the coasts of Africa was completed and some knowledge gained of the interior.

In West Africa, the British and French explored some distance up the Gambia and Senegal rivers; and, later, short distances were ascended up a network of rivers called the Oil Rivers which flowed out to the Guinea coast and were known to Europeans as a market for slaves and palm oil.

The Portuguese were active in the Congo region and, farther south, began to establish themselves in Angola. They also set up trading posts along the east coast and began to penetrate inland. The kingdom of Ethiopia became the goal of Portuguese missionary activities; and among the missionaries were some notable travellers. The outstanding figures were the Jesuits Pedro Paez and Jerome Lobo. Paez was a man of tremendous character. For some years he had been held prisoner by Muslims in Arabia; but in 1603 he arrived in Ethiopia eager to spread the Gospel, having penetrated inland from the coast. The mission was highly successful, for the Emperor himself and his court became converts to Christianity. In 1613 Father Paez accompanied the Emperor and his army on manœuvres, which took them to some springs of water to the south of Lake Tana, a lake which had been known to the ancient Egyptians. Father Paez was quick to understand the significance of these springs. 'I ascended the place,' he declared, 'and observed everything with great attention. As I was looking round about me . . . I discovered two round springs, one of which might be about two feet diameter: the sight filled me with a pleasure which I knew not how to express, when I considered that it was what [the ancients] had so ardently and so much in vain desired to behold.' Father Paez also noted that 'the two openings of these fountains have no issue in the plain on the top of the mountain, but flow from the foot of it. The second fountain lies about a stonecast west from the first'. He went on to give a careful and detailed account of the swampy area and the country surrounding it.

Pedro Paez had, in fact, come upon the source of the Blue Nile, which unites with the parent stream at Khartoum and which is the cause of the Nile floods. His fellow-missionary Father Lobo, having failed in an attempt to find a direct route into Ethiopia from Malindi on the east coast, entered the country from the Red Sea coast and travelled widely. Opinions differ as to whether or not he actually saw the source of the Blue Nile; but his claim to have visited its magnificent waterfall (the Tisisat Falls) was violently disputed for many years. The waterfall thunders from a cliff top into the gorge beneath; and Father Lobo claimed that he was able to get between the cliff and the curtain of pouring water to perch on a rocky ledge on the river bed. From this point, he said, he watched 'a thousand rainbows' formed by the sunlight on the cataract.

Paez, Lobo and other Portuguese missionaries learned much about the interior of Ethiopia; but before very long the missionaries were driven out of the country. In 1699, nearly a hundred years later, another party of missionaries arrived in company with a French doctor, Jacques Charles Poncet, who had been appointed ambassador to the Emperor of Ethiopia by King Louis XIV. Starting from Cairo, the party travelled through Egypt and the Sudan to Sennar on the Blue Nile. Sennar was the capital of the fabulous Fung Empire, which covered most of the territory of the modern Sudan. The origins of the Fung people were unknown; but they had inter-married with the Arabs and adopted the Muslim faith.

The Fungs were said to draw their wealth from gold mines on the Ethiopian border; and the rich merchants of Sennar carried on a trade with India through a port on the Red Sea. Poncet described his journey and also the city and its inhabitants. The women, he wrote, were exotic figures, dressed in vivid silks, wearing silver rings and bangles, their faces stained with kohl. The king, a great property owner, went in procession every week to one or other of his country palaces. The market-place was thronged with merchandise, with slaves, camels, fruit, and a variety of other goods.

In 1701 a missionary from Bavaria, Theodore Krump, followed Poncet's route through Egypt and confirmed his description of Sennar. Poncet, meanwhile, had crossed the river and journeyed on to Gondar, the capital of Ethiopia, above Lake Tana. At Gondar he was called in to attend the Emperor, who was sick. He returned to Europe by way of the Ethiopian port of Massawa on the Red Sea.

A long silence followed Poncet's departure. Missionaries still contrived to reach Ethiopia; but they were not encouraged to settle, and those who did not die from disease soon drifted away. Seventy years were to pass before the source of the Blue Nile was seen by another European. The mystery of the source of the main stream remained unsolved, although expeditions were made into the Nile valley. In 1737 Frederick Norden, a Dane, and an Englishman, Richard Pococke, travelling independently from Cairo, managed to get up the river as far as Philae above Aswan. Norden made drawings and engravings of the antiquities. Other travellers followed them into the Nile valley, but they produced no worth-while information.

In the southern part of the continent the early Portuguese settlements disappeared with the decline of Portuguese power in the sixteenth century; but during the seventeenth century British and Dutch ships began to use the harbour at the Cape of Good Hope as a half-way house on the long voyage to the East Indies. In 1652 the Dutch occupied the site of Cape Town and founded a permanent settlement. During the early years of the eighteenth century they sent expeditions up the south-east coast as far as Natal and Delagoa Bay in search of new areas for settlement: and gradually they began to explore inland towards the Orange River.

III

James Bruce in Ethiopia

IN 1768 A strong, powerfully built Scotsman, six foot four in height, with red hair and a very loud voice, set forth on his African travels. His name was James Bruce, and his family claimed descent from Scotland's ancient King Robert Bruce. He was born in Kinnaird in 1730, heir to the family estates. He was only two years old when his mother died: his father married again and had nine more children. At eight, the boy was sent south to London to school. He was intelligent and studious, and, according to his teacher, 'he inclined to the profession of clergyman for which he has sufficient gravity'. His father, however, insisted that he should study Law, which the boy detested; and so, after a period of study for the Scots Bar at Edinburgh University and a year or two spent at home, Bruce returned to London and a post with the East India Company and the possibility of a career in India or the Far East.

In London he changed his mind. He had fallen in love with a girl whose widowed mother was carrying on her late husband's business as a wine merchant, and when he and the girl were married he was given a partnership in the family firm. Bruce adored his young wife, but after nine rapturously happy months she died, leaving him disconsolate. In his despair, he decided that life would only be bearable if he said goodbye to all the places he knew and achieved something really great. His thoughts turned to the continent of Africa, still largely unknown, and the mystery of the River Nile. His partnership in the wine business gave him an excuse to visit the wine-growing countries, and he spent the next few years in travel and study. First, he learnt Spanish and Portuguese, then Arabic, and later he turned to Amharic, the ancient language of Ethiopia (or Abyssinia as it was then called). He also studied architecture and drawing, for which he had a decided talent; and on a visit to Italy he made the first accurate drawings of the exquisite Greek temples at Paestum.

This was all by way of preparation. In 1763 he took the first step towards his goal. The Government of King George III appointed him British Consul at Algiers in North Africa, which was then part of the Turkish Empire, and gave him permission to travel in Algeria and Tunisia to make drawings of the Roman remains. The King was a great collector; and the drawings were intended for the royal collection.

Before he left home Bruce became engaged to be married to a sixteen-year-old Scots girl, who rashly promised to wait for him. She had no idea—and neither had he—that it would be nearly twelve years before he saw Scotland again, by which time she had given him up for dead and married some one else.

Conditions in Algiers were alarming, to say the least of it. The Bey, the Turkish governor, was vicious and cruel; anybody who annoyed him was either killed, tortured, or flung into prison. Even the consuls, the representatives of foreign powers, were not immune from imprisonment, and Bruce never felt safe: but he put up with these difficult conditions for several years, spending his free time perfecting his Arabic and making ready for his travels. He learned enough medicine to pass as a doctor; and he bought some scientific apparatus, including telescopes, a heavy quadrant, and a portable camera-obscura, in which he could see the image of surrounding objects thrown on a screen. In Algiers he was joined by Luigi Balugani, a young Italian artist, who was to act as his secretary and help him with his drawings for the King's collection. Both men made some exquisite drawings; but Balugani's were the more professional.

At length, in 1768, Bruce received the longed-for permission of the British Government to start on his travels, and in the early summer he left Algiers for Alexandria. He was now on the threshold of his great adventure. He wore Arab dress and he spoke only Arabic; and he posed as a physician and philosopher. He had, however, armed himself with a decree from the Sultan of Egypt describing him as a noble Englishman, a servant of King George III; and while he was in Egypt, practising as a doctor, he persuaded some of his influential patients to give him letters of recommendation to important men on the Red Sea coasts and in Ethiopia. One of these letters was addressed to the ruler of Massawa, the port for Ethiopia; another was to the King of Sennar.

Bruce was leaving nothing to chance. He was already skilled in the use of firearms, and he equipped himself with pistols, guns and blunderbusses. He bought paper for drawing and writing; and, having read everything he could about the Nile, he tore all the relevant pages out of his books and took them with him. He then engaged porters and hired a ship to take him from Cairo up the Nile as far as the first cataract at Aswan.

All this he did entirely at his own expense. He had no desire to plant the British flag on unknown territory; to convert Muslims or pagans to Christianity; or to open up a highway for trade. His motives were purely scientific: he was determined to reveal the secrets of the source of the Nile and to find out as much as possible about the country and its people. He did not know that from the point of view of geography he was in search of the wrong river; for he was convinced that the Blue Nile was really the main stream. And, although he knew all about the claims of Fathers Paez and Lobo, he was more than ready to discount them.

Bruce followed Norden and Pococke's route as far as Aswan, stopping on the way to examine the remains of ancient Thebes. Farther south, the way to the interior was barred by warring tribes; and so he decided to go overland to the coast and join a ship which would eventually land him at Massawa on the Red Sea. In April, 1769, the ship sailed from the busy, squalid little port of Cosseir, to spend the next few months zig-zagging across the Red Sea, calling at various capes and islands. Bruce, who wanted to have a look at the Gulf of Suez and decide for himself exactly how the Children of Israel had contrived to cross from Egypt into Sinai, recorded many useful details about navigation on the Red Sea, where ships frequently foundered. Food and firewood on board were in very short supply and there were times when Bruce and his party had nothing to eat but a mixture of flour and cold water.

In September, five months after the voyage began, the ship docked at Massawa, once the principal port for Ethiopia. The governor, a villainous looking local chieftain, had been warned of Bruce's impending arrival and, imagining that he must be a wealthy relation of King George III, plotted to rob and, if need be, to kill him. Fortunately, Bruce was able to brandish the Sultan's decree which acted as a passport. Even so, he was kept in semi-captivity for two months before he could persuade the governor to let him go. On November 15th, 1769, he left for the interior. With him were the artist Balugani and a party of some 20 men, including a Muslim merchant and a dark-skinned Ethiopian named Yasin.

The route was rough and mountainous: and Bruce, who with Yasin's help was carrying the head of the heavy quadrant, reached the top of the escarpment with his feet torn and bleeding. But he forgot about his trials in the excitement of camping for the first time on Ethiopian soil.

Ethiopia formed a plateau over 6,000 feet high, divided by river valleys and mountain ranges. Bruce and his party, who had climbed the eastern escarpment, came to Adowa, one of its chief strongholds. The name Abyssinia is derived from an Arabic word meaning 'confusion'; and if this was originally meant to imply a confusion of races it could equally well represent the confusion of chaos and civil war in which the country was plunged, and the confusion of savage customs and nominally Christian worship. The throne was held by a ruler who claimed descent from Solomon, son of David. But the power of the Emperor—the King of Kings—had diminished until the government was virtually divided among a number of

provincial governors whose perpetual quarrels and revolts
against the monarchy were the cause of the chaos. The strongest
man in the country was not the Emperor but the Ras (or
Vizier) Michael, Governor of the Province of Tigré. Ras
Michael had already been instrumental in causing the death
of two Emperors, one by assassination, one by poisoning, and
was now ruling in the name of a third, the young Tecla
Haimanot.

The most important house in Adowa was the palace from
which Ras Michael governed Tigré. It was more like a prison
than a house, for nearby were several hundred people in chains.
Some of them had been kept in captivity for twenty years or
more on the off-chance that their families, touched by their
misery, would be able to ransom them. Many were kept in
cages and treated like wild beasts.

Ras Michael and the Emperor were away fighting when
Bruce reached Adowa; and so he pushed on towards Axum,
the ancient capital of Ethiopia. Just outside the ruined city he
overtook three Ethiopian soldiers who were driving a cow before
them. They stopped, and he thought they were about to
slaughter the animal. Instead, they cut some flesh from it,
pinned the wound together and covered it with clay; and then,
so he noted, 'forced the animal to rise, and drove it on before
them, to furnish them with a fuller meal when they should meet
their companions in the evening.' Bruce added, 'I could not yet
conceive that this was the ordinary banquet of the citizens, even
of priests, throughout the country. . . .'

It took Bruce and his companions three months to climb all
the mountain barriers between Massawa and Gondar, the
capital. At Gondar, a city of clay huts with pointed roofs, with a
walled palace overlooking Lake Tana far below, Bruce was
given a house in the Muslim quarter. Ras Michael and the
Emperor were still away; and Bruce found that the people were
dying in hundreds from smallpox and other fevers. This was
scarcely surprising, for the native 'cures' ranged from a medicine made of tinplate and ink to the application of a cross and

a picture of the Virgin Mary. Ras Michael's baby son was desperately sick with smallpox and so were a number of children belonging to the royal family. Bruce, who had already been caring for patients in the Muslim quarter, was now called in to treat the children. He refused unless he was allowed to use his own methods. 'The smallpox,' he said, 'is a disease that will have its course, and during the long time the patient is under it, if people feed him and treat him according to their own ignorant prejudices, my seeing him or advising him is in vain.'

The children were so sick that Bruce was readily given permission to do anything he wished. He found them lying in hot, airless rooms, under mounds of blankets. The first thing he did was to open the doors and windows and wash the walls with vinegar and warm water. He insisted on the strictest rules of hygiene and plenty of fresh air. In due course the children recovered; and by his simple methods Bruce prevented the infection from spreading.

His success won him the gratitude and friendship of Princess Esther, Ras Michael's young and beautiful wife, the mother of the baby and, by a previous marriage, of two of the other children. Princess Esther's beauty can be seen in one of the engravings in the book which Bruce later wrote, *Travels to Discover the Source of the Nile*. She was charming and intelligent as well, and Bruce admitted that he found it impossible to be with her for long 'without being attached to her for ever'.

But, delightful as he found the Princess, Bruce was impatient to press on towards the Blue Nile, which the Ethiopians called Abai—'the father of waters'. The river was not far distant; but he could not go on with his quest without Ras Michael's permission. When the Ras and the Emperor returned from the wars they were greatly impressed by the towering Scotsman, who had had his red hair 'cut round, curled and perfumed in the Amharic fashion', and was dressed, 'like a perfect Abyssinian', in a cloak over chain-armour, with pistols stuck in his wide belt. They admired his conversation, his brilliant horsemanship, his skill at swordplay and shooting. Above all, perhaps, they admired his commanding manner and his confidence, for, in a country where violent death was commonplace, he showed absolutely no fear. So charmed were they by this visitor from another world that they kept putting off Bruce's departure, and the days passed pleasantly enough in hunting and short scientific expeditions. Bruce knew that the Ras was cruel and tyrannical, but even at their first meeting he found him strangely impressive, with his white hair 'dressed in many short curls', his thoughtful air, lean face, and quick, vivid eyes. He found the young Emperor intelligent and handsome, 'not so dark in complexion as a Neopolitan or Portuguese', and with the 'manners and carriage' of a prince.

After delaying Bruce as long as they could the Ras and the Emperor offered to take him on their next expedition to the country south of Lake Tana. There, a chief named Fasil, who belonged to one of the fierce pagan Galla tribes, had been raising an army against them. This was the very region that Bruce longed to explore, but before he could get near the source of the river Fasil surrendered. Bruce managed, however, to reach the river near the point from which it flowed out of Lake Tana, and he then turned south-east towards the great cataract, the Tisisat Falls. Half a mile downstream the river was spanned by a single-arched stone bridge, which had been erected under Portuguese direction a hundred years earlier. Long before he came to the bridge Bruce could hear the thunder of the waterfall. 'The cataract itself,' he wrote,

was the most magnificent sight that I ever beheld. The height has been rather exaggerated. The missionaries say the fall is about sixteen ells, or fifty feet. The measuring is indeed very difficult; but . . . I may venture to say, that it is nearer forty feet than any other measure. The river had been considerably increased by rains, and fell in one sheet of water, without any interval, above half an English mile in breadth, with a force and noise that was truly terrible, and which stunned, and made me, for a time, perfectly dizzy. A thick fume, or haze, covered the fall all round, and hung over the course of the stream both above and below, marking its track, though the water was not seen. It was a magnificent sight that ages, added to the greatest length of human life, would not efface or eradicate from my memory. . . . It was one of the most magnificent, stupendous sights in the creation, much degraded and vilified by the lies of a grovelling fanatic priest.

The 'grovelling fanatic priest' was, of course, Father Lobo. Bruce, who was himself fanatically determined to be the first European to set eyes on the Tisisat Falls, did everything he could to discredit his story. He had two arguments to support his own claim. The first was that Father Lobo had over-estimated the depth of the waterfall, although, as he himself confessed, 'I could at no time in my life less promise upon precision'. In fact, both his own estimate and the missionary's were later proved to be inaccurate, Father Lobo's being nearer the truth. His second argument was that Father Lobo could not possibly have got between the curtain of streaming water and the cliff and that therefore he was lying when he claimed to have discovered the waterfall. Bruce, a powerful swimmer, would not have attempted to find a passage through the water at the foot of the cataract and he was convinced that no one else could have done so. In this, too, he made a mistake; for he saw the falls in the rainy season, while Father Lobo had seen them in the dry season. It was not until the 1920s, however, that it was proved conclusively that during the dry season it is not at all difficult to reach a rocky seat behind the falls, just as Father Lobo had claimed.

Bruce was obliged now to return with the Emperor's army to Gondar, where the prisoners of war were ruthlessly mutilated or killed. He was sick for a time with fever, but in October, 1770, he was at last free to begin his search. He took with him the artist Balugani, a Greek named Strates who lived in Ethiopia, and porters to carry the quadrant. Ras Michael had advised the Emperor to appoint Bruce governor of Gish, the district in which the springs of the Blue Nile were known to rise. Gish was still dominated by Fasil, the rebellious Galla chief, whose tribesmen were once again raiding the countryside in the direction of Gondar, and Bruce could not pass without the chieftain's permission. He found Fasil encamped with his army to the north-west of Lake Tana. Fasil received him, squatting on a lion's skin in his tent. His head was wound in 'a cotton cloth something like a dirty towel': his greasy cloak was wrapped so tightly about him that when Bruce stepped forward to pay him the usual courtesy of hand kissing his lips merely brushed the cloth.

Although Fasil was well aware that Bruce's appointment had been made with the sole object of enabling him to visit the source of the Blue Nile he disclaimed all knowledge of its whereabouts. 'Do you know what you are saying?' he cried. 'The source of the Abai! Why, it is God knows where in the country of the Galla, wild, terrible people. Are you mad? It might take you a year to get back.'

Bruce, after reminding Fasil that it was well known that the Nile source lay within his territory, tried flattery. 'It was relying upon you alone that I came so far,' he said, 'confident if all the rest of Abyssinia could not protect me, then your word alone could do it.'

Fasil was slightly mollified, but he remained obdurate. 'I found now,' wrote Bruce, 'as I thought, that . . . my hopes of arriving at the source of the Nile were for ever ended; all my trouble, all my expense, all my time, and all my sufferings for so many years, were thrown away, from no greater obstacle than the whimsies of one barbarian.'

Where argument and pleading had failed, however, Bruce captivated the chieftain by his skill in subduing wild horses and his ability to shoot kites on the wing. Fasil gave way. He lent Bruce his own horse, telling him to drive it before him, saddled and bridled, as a sign of his favour—a sign which all his people would understand and respect. He also provided him with a guide and the rather doubtful protection of seven minor chiefs, of whom Bruce wrote, 'I never saw more thief-like fellows in my life.'

Thus equipped Bruce went forward on the last phase of his search. The party skirted the western shore of Lake Tana and pushed on towards the south. They passed through an easy, pleasant piece of country with a distant view of mountains, and bright with 'trees and shrubs covered with flowers of every colour, all new and extraordinary in their shape, crowded with birds of many uncouth forms, all of them richly adorned with a variety of plumage . . . At two o'clock in the afternoon of the second of November,' he noted, 'we came to the banks of the Nile'. Two days later he reached the climax of his adventure. With his companions he climbed a mountain which had a little church on its summit; and, gazing down, 'we saw, immediately below us, the Nile itself, strangely diminished in size, and now only a brook that had scarcely water to turn a mill. I could not satiate myself with the sight, revolving in my mind all those classical prophecies that had given the Nile up to perpetual obscurity and concealment. . . .'

The guide then pointed beyond the church to a little swamp. ' "Look at that hillock of green sod in the middle of that watery spot," he said. "The two springs of the Nile are there. If you go to them, pull off your shoes . . ., for the people here are all pagans . . . They believe in nothing that you believe, but only in this river, to which they pray every day as if it were God—but perhaps you will do as much yourself?" '

Pausing only to pull off his shoes, Bruce stumbled down the hillside 'towards the little island of green sods . . .; the whole side of the hill was thick overgrown with flowers, the large bulbous roots of which appearing over the surface of the ground, and their skins coming off on treading upon them, occasioned me two very severe falls before I reached the brink of the marsh.' He picked himself up and then 'came to the island of green turf, which was in form of an altar . . . I stood in rapture over the principal fountain which rises in the middle of it.'

If Bruce did not actually worship the river he was filled with

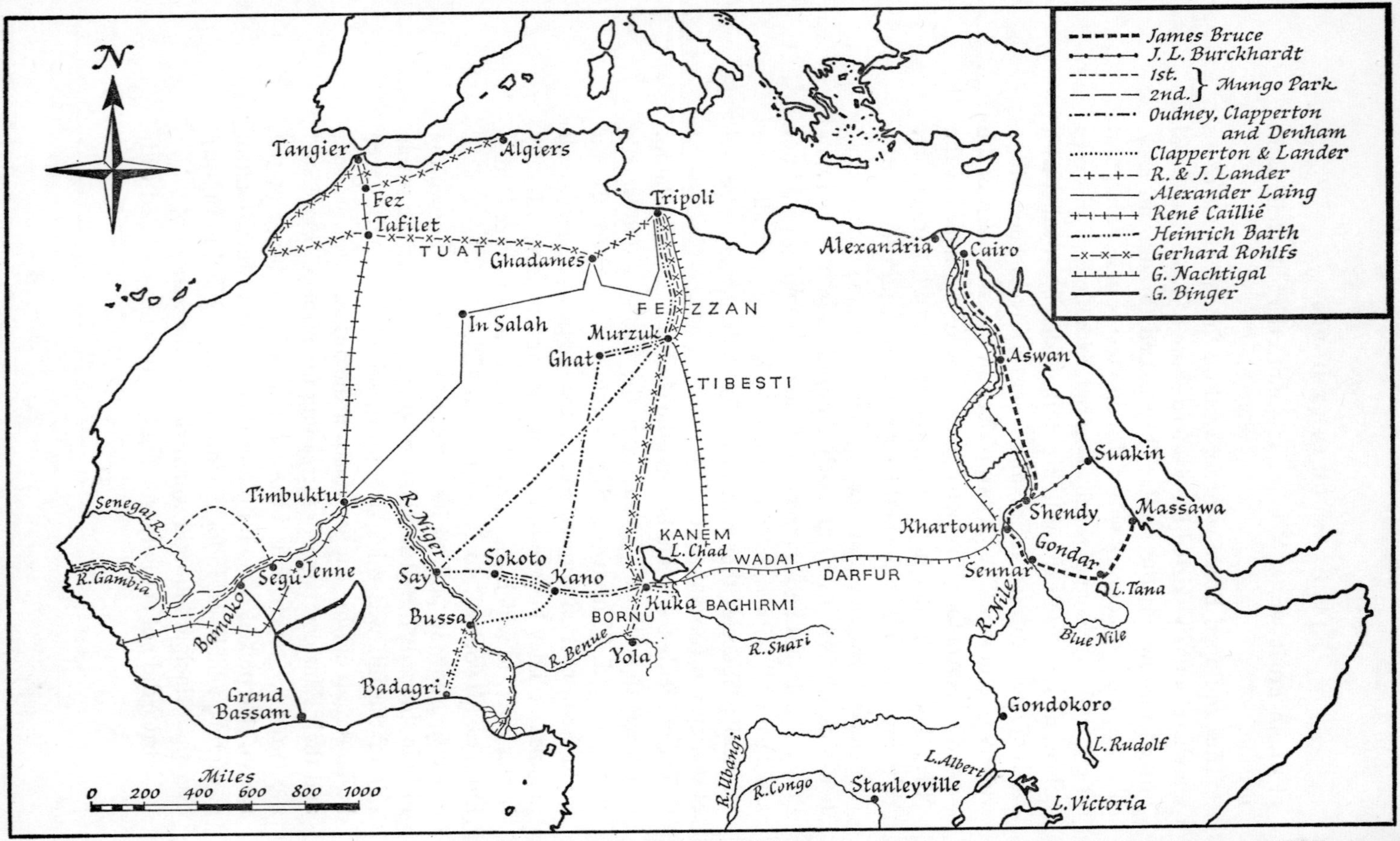

Legend:

- James Bruce
- J. L. Burckhardt
- Mungo Park (1st.)
- Mungo Park (2nd.)
- Oudney, Clapperton and Denham
- Clapperton & Lander
- R. & J. Lander
- Alexander Laing
- René Caillié
- Heinrich Barth
- Gerhard Rohlfs
- G. Nachtigal
- G. Binger

N

Tangier
Algiers
Fez
Tafilet
TUAT
Ghadames
In Salah
Tripoli
Murzuk
Ghat
FEZZAN
TIBESTI
Alexandria
Cairo
Aswan
Suakin
Massawa
Shendy
Gondar
L. Tana
Khartoum
Sennar
Blue Nile
R. Nile
DARFUR
WADAI
KANEM
L. Chad
BORNU
Kuka
BAGHIRMI
R. Shari
Gondokoro
L. Rudolf
L. Victoria
L. Albert
Stanleyville
R. Congo
R. Ubangi
Kano
Sokoto
Yola
R. Benue
Say
Bussa
Badagri
R. Niger
Timbuktu
Segu
Jenne
Bamako
Grand Bassam
Senegal R.
R. Gambia

Miles
0 200 400 600 800 1000

FIG. 1. ROUTES IN NORTHERN AFRICA

exaltation. 'It is easier to guess than to describe the situation of my mind at that moment,' he continued, 'standing in that spot which had baffled the genius, industry and inquiry of both ancients and moderns, for the course of near three thousand years . . . Though a mere private Briton,' he added with pride, 'I triumphed here in my own mind, over kings and their armies.'

In ignoring the very just claims of Father Paez, who had undoubtedly visited the same spot 150 years earlier, Bruce was pitching his own claims far too high; but, so determined was he to be first on the scene, that he was able to delude himself into the belief that he was. Moreover, if he had been searching for the true source of the Nile he had not found it. The Blue Nile, which provides so much of the Nile waters, is, in fact, only a great tributary of the White Nile, whose source lies 1,000 miles away.

Reaction followed Bruce's moment of triumph, and he thought of the long journey before him. But in a spirit of bravado he picked up half a coconut and drank a toast in Nile water to King George III, inviting Strates, the Greek, to drink with him. There is no record in Bruce's book that Balugani was also invited to drink, although there is no doubt that the artist was with him. Balugani died of dysentery at Gondar on the homeward journey; but in his determination to keep the glory for himself, Bruce pretended that the artist was dead before the Nile search began. Strates, who lived in Ethiopia, was no rival; but Bruce ungenerously consigned Balugani and Fathers Paez and Lobo to limbo.

After spending several days examining and measuring the area Bruce made his way back to Gondar. In his absence Galla tribesmen had attacked the city in force; and Bruce himself fought at the head of a band of the Emperor's Guard. He was a brilliant shot; and his services as a doctor were in great demand among the wounded. The rebels were defeated; and Bruce was forced to witness the dreadful vengeance of Ras Michael. He protested in vain at the barbarity of the executions.

' "Is it really possible that you take such things as these to heart?" asked the Ras. "You are a brave man; we all know you are, and have seen it; we have all blamed you, stranger as you are in this country, for the little care you take of yourself; and yet about these things you are as much affected as the most cowardly woman, girl, or child could be." "Sir," ' answered Bruce, ' "I do not know if I am brave or not; but if to see men tortured, or murdered, or to live among dead bodies without concern, be courage, I have it not. . . ." '

Before he left Ethiopia Bruce spent several months studying the people and the history and geography of their country in what has since proved to be an extremely accurate manner. He also made a valuable collection of Amharic documents, plants and minerals which he planned to take back to Europe. And then, having extracted permission to leave, he bade farewell to the beautiful Princess Esther and the little boy whose life he he had saved. They were now living in retirement; and Bruce described the meeting as 'one of the happiest moments of my life'.

In December, 1771, he left Ethiopian soil and, travelling westward, entered the strange Empire of the Fung. The Empire was made up of a number of small states: and the people, who belonged to different tribes and races, ranged in colour from light brown to ebony. Bruce, who described everything he saw with the utmost care, was the first European to record the ravages of the tsaltsalya fly, an insect as dangerous as the tsetse fly, whose bite infected animals with a deadly disease and forced the herdsmen to leave their pasture lands for the sparse wet-season vegetation of the desert, where the flies did not breed.

The first stage of the journey was through semi-desert country. The weather grew steadily hotter. By March the streams and waterholes were almost dry, and animals, weakened by hunger and thirst, were an easy prey for the lions and hyenas which lurked in the bush. Presently the party came to a stretch of treeless desert and to a deserted village whose population had been wiped out the previous year when the scanty

JAMES BRUCE IN ETHIOPIA

crops failed. 'We encamped among the bones of the dead,' wrote Bruce. 'No space could be found free of them.' It had taken them a week to march 65 miles: but they were now nearing the bed of a river which had not run dry and a town, Teawa.

Sheikh Fidele, the ebony-skinned governor of Teawa, greeted them with outward friendliness; but Bruce was warned that he was 'a devil' who would do his utmost to stop them from going on to Sennar, capital of the Fung Empire. Bruce, who gave his usual demonstration of fine horsemanship and shooting, might well have lost his life but for his medical powers. He prescribed successfully for Fidele and for his wives and daughters; and when the Sheikh showed signs of hostility towards Bruce the women intervened on his behalf. Bruce thoroughly enjoyed flirting with the women. 'Being in the prime of life,' he wrote, 'of no ungracious figure, having an accidental knack, which is not a trifle, of putting on the dress and speaking the language easily and gracefully, I cultivated with the utmost assiduity the friendship of the fair sex, by the most modest, respectful, distant attendance and obsequiousness in public, abating just as much of that in private as suited their humour and inclinations.'

Presumably Bruce did not proceed far enough to arouse Fidele's jealousy; but the Shiekh obstinately refused to let him go. He owed his release to his first Ethiopian friend, Yasin, who had left him to return to his own village. When Yasin heard of Bruce's predicament, he sent three mail-clad soldiers with letters threatening to destroy Teawa and burn down the crops if Bruce were not allowed to go free. Fidele gave way; and Bruce, with a gesture of apparent generosity, presented him with his horse: he had been warned that horses could not live in Sennar! Then he departed thankfully, travelling by night to escape the burning heat of day.

The Frenchman Poncet and the German Krump had, of course, already visited Sennar seventy years earlier. Poncet had been impressed with the size and importance of the city; but Bruce found it grim and oppressive. He arrived during the dry

35

season when the incidence of disease and death was particularly high; and he noted that only by the importation of captured slaves from the south could the population be maintained. He disliked the people, finding them sullen and suspicious. 'War and treason,' he wrote, 'seem to be the only employment of this horrid people whom Heaven has separated by almost impassable deserts from the rest of mankind, confining them to an accursed spot. . . .'

Bruce was presented to the King, a weak, indolent young man, brown-skinned like his Arab mother, and with 'a very plebeian countenance on which was stamped no decided character . . .' The King was astonished to learn that Bruce had chosen to spend so many years in Africa. ' "How is it," he asked, "that you, who are so noble and learned that you know everything and speak all languages, and so brave that you are not afraid to travel with a few old men through countries like this one and Ethiopia, have not stayed at home to enjoy yourself, eat, drink and take pleasure instead of wandering like a poor man exposed to all sorts of dangers?" '

By way of explanation Bruce replied that he was a sort of dervish, pledged to lead a life of austerity and poverty, 'bound to travel in hardships and danger, doing all the good I can to poor and rich and hurting nobody.' When he told the King that he had been travelling for so many years the King came to the conclusion that he must have committed a great many sins when he was very young to have had to spend so long expiating them. Had the sins all been with women, he wanted to know. Some of them probably were, Bruce replied with becoming modesty. This answer satisfied the King, who invited Bruce to sit on a cushion during the rest of the interview. Later in the day Bruce returned bringing presents; and he watched while one of the King's servants rubbed his master with stinking elephant's fat, which was supposed to make him strong and keep his skin smooth. The King suggested that Bruce should try the treatment: it might, he thought, prevent his hair from growing so red!

James Bruce

Mungo Park

John Lewis Burckhardt

As in Ethiopia, the dominant figure of Sennar was not the King but a minister, Sheikh Adelan, who had a magnificent troop of Arab horses and an army of horsemen decked out in helmets and coats of mail. But, despite this show of power, the Fung Empire was in the same state of chaos and civil war as Ethiopia. Bruce was thankful to get away from Sennar, but he was not allowed to leave until most of his belongings had been taken from him.

It was now September, 1772. He was on his way to the White Nile and to Cairo, 2,000 miles down river. It took him only three weeks to reach the meeting-place of the White Nile and the Blue, at Khartoum. He noted that the White Nile was very deep and that its flow was more consistently great than that of the Blue Nile. 'Rising in latitudes where there are continual rains,' he wrote, 'it suffers not the decrease the Nile does by the six months' dry weather.' Whatever the evidence to the contrary, Bruce persisted in calling his own river 'the Nile'. According to his reckoning, the Blue Nile was the main stream; the White Nile the tributary.

By this time, despite his physical strength and undoubted courage, Bruce was feeling tired and dispirited. To make things worse, he became infected with guinea worm, a parasitic disease which developed in his leg and made walking a penance. When, therefore, he reached the little market-town of Shendy in October he settled down for a couple of weeks. Nearby he discovered the remains of an ancient settlement, and he passed the time examining the ruins and paying court to the Queen of Shendy, an exotic-looking woman of forty. The Queen was flustered but pleased when Bruce kissed her hand. ' "Do you know," she exclaimed, "that no man has ever kissed my hand but you?" "It was meant respectfully," ' replied Bruce, and he explained that in England this greeting was reserved for kings and queens, which pleased her still more. In fact, she was so flattered that she offered Bruce a guide; and at the end of the month he went on his way with a party of nine, riding on camels. As they journeyed on they passed some ruins which

37

Bruce assumed correctly were those of ancient Meroe, capital of Nubia, which, according to legend, was founded by Moses in honour of Pharaoh's daughter Merr who had adopted him.

Before crossing the Atbara River, the last of the Nile's tributaries, the party rested and Bruce bought more camels. He now faced a desert crossing of some 400 miles, having chosen it in preference to the longer route which followed the course of the Nile. On November 11th, while the camels were being loaded, Bruce bathed in the Nile, 'and thus took leave of my old acquaintance, very doubtful if we should ever meet again.'

The desert journey was a nightmare of heat and sandstorms. Bruce's leg troubled him, his neck was covered in blisters, his feet swollen and bleeding. One by one the camels died; and when the party reached a water-hole the chances were that it would be filled with dead animals. Eighteen days later they struggled thankfully into Aswan and sailed down the Nile to Cairo.

Before returning to England Bruce spent several months in Europe. In Italy, he stormed into the presence of the Italian nobleman who had, as he now knew, married the girl he had left behind him in Scotland and challenged the unfortunate man to a duel. The Italian, who had never even heard of Bruce, wrote a hasty apology for having wronged him unwittingly; and Bruce departed, to arrive in London in June, 1774, after an absence of twelve years.

He created a sensation in fashionable circles. 'All Europe will not furnish me with another paragraph,' declared the well known writer Horace Walpole. 'Africa is indeed coming into fashion. There is just returned a Mr Bruce who has lived three years in the Court of Abyssinia, and breakfasted every morning with the maids of honour on live oxen.'

Bruce's stories of his adventures were considered fantastic and for the most part they were disbelieved. George III granted him an audience and graciously accepted the drawings which he and Balugani had made; but Bruce received no official recognition, and the learned societies were extremely sceptical about his claim to have discovered the source of the Nile.

One of his chief adversaries was the celebrated Dr Johnson, by now an old man. Johnson, whose own book *Rasselas, Prince of Abyssinia*, presented an idealised Ethiopia very different from the truth, had translated into English Father Lobo's *A Voyage to Abyssinia*. He admired the Jesuit and was furious when Bruce called him a liar and a fraud. In reply, Johnson declared that Bruce was utterly unreliable.

Hurt and mortified by his cool reception Bruce retired to his Scottish estates and to a brief and happy marriage. When his young wife died a friend prevailed on him to try and forget his unhappiness by writing an account of his adventures. His book, *Travels to Discover the Source of the Nile*, was published in 1790, seventeen years after his return from Africa, and it can be read today with tremendous enjoyment. Bruce suspected that the book would lead to trouble. In a preface he declared that he would not answer 'any cavills, captious or idle objection' which might be levelled against him. 'What I have written I have written,' he said.

He was right about the trouble. The book was mercilessly pulled to pieces by the critics: his stories were ridiculed; and many people refused to believe that he had ever been in Ethiopia, much less visited the source of the Nile.

Sullen and indignant Bruce retired once more into his shell, to die in 1779 at the age of sixty-four, in the knowledge that his contemporaries had judged him unfairly.

The argument about the rights and wrongs of Bruce's account of his adventures continued, and even today there are people who believe that he was a liar. In fact, while his book contains certain exaggerations and inconsistencies, later travellers and explorers found that in its essentials it was sound and accurate; and there is no doubt at all that he travelled in Ethiopia and visited the source of the Blue Nile. It is a great pity that his pride and ambition led him to blacken the names of Fathers Paez and Lobo and to conceal the fact that Balugani also saw the fountains of the Blue Nile. This was a grave defect in a man who was brave and resourceful, generous, warm-hearted and humane.

And yet, if Bruce had only confirmed what other men had seen, he had travelled widely and had produced a wealth of immensely valuable information. In this way he opened a path for the travellers who came after him: and he has with truth been called the first great scientific explorer of Africa.

IV

Mungo Park and the Niger

BRUCE WAS STILL on his travels when the first shots were fired in the long fight against the slave trade in which the nations of Europe had so eagerly taken part. In 1772 the Lord Chief Justice of England, Lord Mansfield, delivered a judgment which had the effect of liberating every slave to set foot on English soil.

The next stage was the abolition of the British slave trade and the start of British intervention in Africa. The abolitionists had to wage a prolonged battle against the bitter opposition of those with vested interests in a continuance of the trade. In 1807, however, an Act of Parliament was passed laying down that after January 1808 'all manner of dealing and trading' in slaves either in Africa or in their transport from Africa to any other place was to be 'utterly abolished, prohibited, and declared to be unlawful'. In 1807 a portion of land, which had been sold by the local king to abolitionists in 1788 to form a colony for a settlement of freed African slaves, became a British Crown Colony.

In the meantime, the authorities were aware that if the African slave trade was to be abolished it must be replaced by trade in legitimate goods: but before the possibilities of trade with the interior of Africa could be properly assessed the country would have to be explored and surveyed.

The foremost patron of African exploration was Sir Joseph Banks, the British scientist who had sailed round the world with Captain Cook. Banks, who was born in 1743 the son of a wealthy landowner, was for upwards of 40 years President of the Royal Society, Britain's oldest and most famous scientific body. He was also a founder member of a club which met every week to dine and discuss scientific subjects. On June 7th, 1788, with Banks himself presiding, the talk turned to Africa and its still unknown interior. Before the evening was over the members had formed themselves into an 'Association for Promoting the Discovery of the Inland Districts of Africa', or the African Association as it came to be called. The objects of the new Association were to build up trade between Britain and West Africa and to trace the course of the Niger, a river which no European had ever seen and on whose banks stood the glittering city of Timbuktu. Some geographers believed that the Niger was a tributary of the Nile, although they could not decide whether it flowed west or east: others thought it must be a branch of the Congo, or even the Congo itself. But these were merely speculations, for British discovery had not yet been carried beyond the Senegal and Gambia Rivers and short distances up the network of the Oil Rivers which flowed out to the Guinea coast.

The first need obviously was to recruit travellers for the interior of West Africa as soon as possible; and the Secretary was pleased when a volunteer who called on him one morning said that he would be ready to start the following day. The volunteer was an adventurous, thirty-seven-year-old American, John Ledyard, who had been born in Groton, Connecticut. When he first came to England, Ledyard had joined the Marines and had sailed with Captain Cook on his last voyage to the South Seas. He had met Sir Joseph Banks who sent him on a hazardous mission to Kamchatka in Siberia; but as he neglected to apply for a permit to remain in Russia, he was thrown out of the country and arrived back in London without a penny in his pocket. The African Association now invited him to go to Egypt and to cross the Libyan Desert to the Niger. Ledyard himself was determined to find Timbuktu, but he got no further than Cairo, where he fell ill and died.

While Ledyard was on his way to Egypt the Association sent a second volunteer, Lucas, to North Africa with instructions to

42

cross the Sahara and push on towards the Niger. All Lucas was able to do was to gather a certain amount of information about the existing trade routes across the desert. A third traveller, Frederick Hornemann, starting from Egypt in 1789, crossed the Libyan Desert to reach Murzuk, an important trading post and capital of the Fezzan; he left Murzuk then disappeared without a trace. A fourth, Major Houghton, landed on the west coast and followed the Gambia River as far as Medina in Senegal; but soon afterwards he was ambushed by tribesmen, robbed and murdered.

After these initial setbacks Banks remembered a young ship's doctor who had brought him an interesting collection of plants from a voyage to the West Indies. The doctor was Mungo Park, born in 1771, the seventh child of a Scottish farmer who lived in Selkirkshire near the River Yarrow. Park, who was educated at the local grammar school, completed his medical studies at the University of Edinburgh. But medical practice in Scotland was too tame to suit the young man's tastes. He was strong and energetic, eager for some enterprise to test his strength and daring; and so he came to London where he was introduced to Banks. When Banks learned that Park wanted to travel he used his influence to get him the post as ship's doctor; and when Park called on him at the conclusion of another voyage Banks invited him to go to West Africa and take up the search for the Niger.

Park was ambitious, and, as Banks guessed, he possessed all the detached curiosity and the powers of accurate observation which mark the true scientist. He accepted the offer at once, and in 1795, at the age of twenty-four, he sailed from Portsmouth, arriving on the Gambia River a month later after an uneventful voyage.

The journey inland, as he well knew, would be far from uneventful; but he had infinite faith in his own capabilities and in the good intentions of the African Association. 'If,' he declared,

I should perish in my journey, I was willing that my hopes

and expectations should perish with me; and if I should succeed in rendering the geography of Africa more familiar to my countrymen, and in opening to their ambition and industry new sources of wealth and new channels of commerce, I knew that I was in the hands of men of honour, who would not fail to bestow that remuneration which my successful services would appear to them to merit.

Before starting his search Park spent several months learning the Mandingo language, spoken over a large area of the interior, for he intended to talk to the people without an interpreter. At the end of the year he left Pisania on the Gambia, taking with him only two African servants and a small amount of equipment. He was dressed, as in his native Scotland, in thick breeches fastened below the knee, a heavy bright blue coat with gilt buttons, and a tall stiff hat. The buttons proved too strong a temptation to be resisted; and before long Park had been robbed of his coat and most of his possessions; but he managed to keep his hat, which he used not so much as a head covering but as a hiding place for his notes on West Africa's peoples, products and trade, plants and animals. He was so thorough and accurate in his observations that nothing he ever set down as fact has since been disputed or disproved.

Everything went well at the start. Park journeyed eastward through small states ruled by Negro kings, whose friendship he won by his ready sympathy, disarming ease of manner, and invariable good temper. But these gentle qualities were reinforced by immense courage. Park was well aware of the fate of his predecessors and he did not blench when he was shown the actual place in the forest where Major Houghton had been murdered.

The kings of these pagan states were often at war with one another, with the sole object of taking prisoners to sell as slaves. The slave trade was almost their only form of trade, and by far the most profitable. Park reckoned that no fewer than three-quarters of all the people he encountered were slaves, either

Sir Joseph Banks

Captain Hugh Clapperton

The Murchison Falls

taken in battle or sold because they had committed some crime or could not pay their debts. But, although the kings robbed and delayed Park, they did him no harm. Indeed, they were so concerned for his safety that they implored him to go no farther.

At Medina, near the spot where Houghton had been killed, the king of the state of Woolli

> tenderly intreated me to desist from my purpose of travelling into the interior, telling me that . . . if I followed [Houghton's] footsteps I should probably meet his fate. He said that I must not judge of the people of the eastern country by those of Woolli; that the latter were acquainted with white men, and respected them; whereas the people of the east had never seen a white man, and would certainly destroy me. I thanked the king for his affectionate solicitude, but told him that I had considered the matter, and was determined, notwithstanding all dangers, to proceed. The king shook his head, but desisted from further persuasion. . . .

The King also provided Park with a guide to help him on the next stage of his journey. Park was making for the Niger; but on the way there was much of interest to observe and note. Soon Park was stopping to examine 'a sort of masquerade habit, made of bark', the property of 'a strange bugbear common to all Mandingo towns', known as Mumbo Jumbo, and used by the men to keep their wives in subjection. As the men

> are not restricted in the number of their wives, every one marries as many as he can conveniently maintain; and as it frequently happens that the ladies disagree among themselves, family quarrels sometimes rise to such a height that the authority of the husband can no longer preserve peace in his household. In such cases the interposition of Mumbo Jumbo is called in, and is always decisive.
> This strange minister of justice (who is supposed to be

either the husband himself or some person instructed by him),
disguised in the dress that has been mentioned, and armed
with the rod of public authority, announces his coming . . .
by loud and dismal screams. . . . He begins his pantomime at
the approach of night . . . and all the inhabitants [of the
town] immediately assemble. . . . The ceremony commences
with songs and dances, which continue till midnight, about
which time Mumbo fixes on the offender. This unfortunate
victim being thereupon immediately seized, is stripped
naked, tied to a post, and severely scourged with Mumbo's
rod, amid the shouts and derision of the whole assembly;
and it is remarkable that the rest of the women are the
loudest in the exclamations on this occasion against their
unhappy sister.

Before crossing the frontier between Woolli and the state of
Bondu Park watched a wrestling match between two champions
and noted the drumming 'by which their actions were in some
measure regulated'. At the dance which followed the match the
drum was 'likewise applied . . . to keep order among the spectators, by imitating the sound of certain Mandingo sentences'.
Park thus anticipated modern theories of the method of convey-
ing messages by African drums: he had detected the fact that
because the drum-beats imitate simple language sounds they
are as clear as the spoken word to any one who understands the
language.

Painstaking and inquiring, Park continued his researches:
the methods used by slave traders to prevent their slaves from
escaping are described in his journal in the same detail as the
technique for sifting gold dust or dyeing cotton cloth with indigo
'an excellent blue'. Even when, later, he was taken prisoner and
surrounded by galloping horsemen twirling muskets round their
heads 'as if they were baiting a wild animal' he calmed himself
by making observations on their horsemanship.

Trouble awaited him beyond the borders of the friendly
pagan states. Modestly re-equipped with the help of a European

trader, he passed into the great Muslim kingdoms, whose people were already seeking to spread the faith of Islam among the pagans. These Muslims (or Moors), part Arab and part Negro, were ruled by sultans or emirs. As soon as Park passed into Muslim-ruled territory he was attacked and robbed. At this point his Negro servants declared that they could go no farther for fear of being taken as slaves. Park went on alone.

If the servants had turned back straight away they might have escaped, but they did not hurry and were captured. Park could not help them, for by this time he too had been captured and was being dragged back along the route he had followed from the frontier. For the rest of his life he was to have a recurrent dream about his subsequent imprisonment by the Moors, who treated him with the utmost cruelty. On one occasion, when he begged for a drink of water at a well, an old man obligingly drew up a bucketful. But as Park was about to take hold of it, the old man, recollecting that he was a Christian, 'and fearing that his bucket might be polluted by my lips', poured the water into a trough at which three cows were already drinking, and Park had to drink with the beasts.

Despite all the petty persecutions he was forced to endure and the knowledge that, but for him, his servants might still be free, Park never lost control of his temper and relaxed his mind with the study of Arabic. Death was never very far away. But for the kindness of some of the women, he would probably have died of starvation if he had not been murdered. The Moors despised him as a Christian and could not believe that he was simply an explorer and not the precursor of an armed invasion. The single attribute they appeared to respect was his magnificent red beard. 'I think, in my conscience,' he wrote, 'they thought it too good a beard for a Christian.'

After nearly three months as a captive Park decided that his sole chance of survival was escape. 'And yet, if I went forward singly, it was evident that I must sustain great difficulties. . . . On the other hand, to return to England, without accomplishing the object of my mission, was worse than either.' And so, with the connivance of one of his former servants who was a prisoner in the same camp, he slipped away when the Moors were sleeping. He had gone scarcely two miles when he heard a shout, and three Moors galloped up, 'whooping and brandishing their double-barrelled guns. . . . When the human mind has for some time been fluctuating between hope and despair,' he added,

> tortured with anxiety, and hurried from one extreme to another, it affords a sort of gloomy relief to know the worst that can possibly happen; such was now my situation. . . .

Fortunately, these Moors merely wanted to rob him not to take him prisoner; and, having taken his small bundle of spare clothing, they let him go. Weakened by hunger, thirst and fever, haunted continually by the fear of recapture, he struggled on, journeying south-eastward. In July, 1796, he joined a party of fugitives from Moorish tyranny and accompanied them to the great market town of Segu on the Niger. And now at last he saw

> the majestic long-sought Niger, glittering in the morning sun, as broad as the Thames at Westminster and flowing slowly *to the eastward*. I hastened to the brink, and having drunk of the water, lifted up my fervent thanks in prayer to the Great Ruler of all things, for having thus far crowned my endeavours with success.

He had not only seen the Niger but he had solved one of the problems which puzzled the geographers of Europe: the river flowed east and not west.

Weary and in rags, but still clutching the tall hat containing his precious notes, Park struggled almost a hundred miles along the north bank of the river in an effort to trace its course. But the rainy season had begun, the river was rising ominously, and he was entirely without resources. To have gone on would have brought him once more into hostile Muslim country, among

48

people whose language he could not speak, and so he gave up, within twelve days' march of Timbuktu.

With the utmost reluctance he turned, to stumble and beg his way 300 miles west to Kamalia. At the very lowest ebb of his fortunes, he was welcomed by a Muslim slaver, Karfa Taura, who kept him for seven months, not as a captive but as an honoured guest, and nursed him through a long bout of fever. When he was fully recovered Park joined Karfa's slave caravan and accompanied it for 500 miles to his starting point on the Gambia. There he was received by his European trader friends 'as one risen from the dead'. Long ago they had given him up for lost, fearing that like Major Houghton he had been murdered.

Park arrived in London on Christmas Day, 1797, and immediately called on Sir Joseph Banks, who was extremely proud of his achievement. The African Association decided to keep Park in its service until he had written up his notes in book form, and he went back to Scotland to his mother, now a widow.

His book, *Travels in the Interior Districts of Africa*, was published in 1799. It was immensely popular and was to prove indispensable to later explorers. By this time Park had married his 'lovely Ailie', the daughter of the surgeon to whom he had been apprenticed, and he himself was now in practice as a doctor. Banks wanted to send him to explore the unknown interior of Australia. Park refused; he was very happily married and for the time being had no desire for further travel.

One morning in 1804, however, a friend—Sir Walter Scott, the famous novelist—rode over the hills to visit the doctor. He found him throwing stones into a deep pool between the rock ledges of the Yarrow, watching the bubbles as they rose to the surface. Lockart, Scott's biographer, described the meeting.

'This,' said Scott, 'appears but an idle amusement for one who has seen so much stirring adventure.' 'Not so idle, perhaps, as you suppose,' answered Mungo Park. 'This was the manner in which I used to ascertain the depth of a river in Africa before I ventured to cross it—judging whether the attempt would be safe, by the time the bubbles of air took to ascend.'

Until this moment Scott had known nothing of Park's intention of tackling a second expedition; but he instantly decided that 'these experiments on Yarrow were connected with some such purpose'.

He was right. Park had already been approached by Lord Camden, the Colonial Secretary, who informed Banks that 'Mr Park . . . appears willing to undertake an Expedition of Enquiry into the interior of Africa, and particularly to endeavour to ascertain the course of the Niger'.

Scott was astounded at his friend's eagerness to face another expedition; but Park's longing to sail down the Niger to its mouth was so strong that neither his dearly loved wife nor his three children could keep him at home. The two men had a farewell ride together, at the end of which Park's horse stumbled over a low ditch. To the novelist this seemed a bad omen, and he said as much. 'Freits [omens] follow those who look for them,' laughed Park: Scott never saw him again.

The explorer's light-hearted attitude, courageous though it sounded, was not justified. He was, in fact, far too light-hearted and casual. The very energy that had driven him to accomplish so much made him impatient of delays, and the optimism that had sustained him in the direst straits made him overconfident. This would seem to be the explanation of the risk he took at the outset. His original plan was to travel overland from the Gambia to the Niger in the dry season and to sail down the river when the rains gave high water and made the rapids passable. But the expedition was being sponsored by the British Government and not the African Association; and in 1804—shortly before the Battle of Trafalgar—the Government was so preoccupied with the possibility that Napoleon might invade England that preparations for Park's journey were postponed. By the time they had been completed Park realised that he could only hope to reach the Niger by the beginning of the rainy season if everything went according to plan. Perhaps he dared not ask for a further delay: perhaps he was too proud to do so, for Banks, who had already stated that the journey would be 'one of the most hazardous ever undertaken', had added that in his opinion the dangers were no greater than might reasonably be faced, since without such hazards great geographical discoveries could never be made.

Banks and his colleagues have sometimes been criticized for the risks they took with the lives of other men. But in his younger days Banks had cheerfully risked his own life in the interests of science; and there never was an expedition which could have been called even reasonably safe. Park himself had no hard feelings. Although he was known to be very reserved and rather cold in manner, his attitude towards the wealthy, influential sponsor, so much his senior in years and importance, was such that he always addressed Banks in letters as 'My dear Friend'.

The final commission was issued on January 2nd, 1805. When he arrived on the West African coast Park wrote home optimistically: 'If Sir Joseph enquires after me, tell him that I'm going on as well as I could wish; and . . . I hope to be able to date a letter from the Niger by the 4th June.'

If Park had been travelling alone he might well have reached the Niger by the beginning of June; but this time he had more than 40 Europeans with him—most of them soldiers—and one or two friends, including his brother-in-law, Alexander Anderson. He realised that travel during the rainy season could have serious consequences to white men; and, as his companions lacked his energy and extraordinary physical stamina, they ran into difficulties almost at once. By the end of April Park wrote to Banks from the Gambia begging him to make sure that if rumours of mishaps reached him they should as far as possible be prevented from 'finding their way into the newspapers or in any other way reaching the ears of my dear wife or mother'.

The rains started in June, but it was not until mid-August that 11 Europeans reached the Niger: the others had died on the way from sunstroke, fever, or dysentery. The sight of the river raised Park's hopes. 'Having gained the summit of the ridge which separates the Niger from the remote branches of the Senegal,' he declared, 'I went on a little before; and coming to the brow of the hill, I *once more saw the Niger* rolling its immense stream along the plain!' Few were now left to share his excitement: six more died before they could reach the unexplored portion of the river, and to Park's sorrow his brother-in-law was one of them. 'No event during the journey ever threw the smallest gloom over my mind till I laid Mr Anderson in the grave. I then felt myself as if left a second time, lonely and friendless, amid the wilds of Africa.'

Whatever his feelings, Park's efforts never slackened. He seemed to the survivors to be everywhere at once, caring for the sick, drying soaked stores, scaring off lions, and chasing robbers. One night he crossed and recrossed a crocodile-infested river no fewer than 16 times, carrying men and loads, and after this escapade merely admitted to feeling 'somewhat fatigued'. When he went down with dysentery he dosed himself so heavily with calomel that he could neither speak nor sleep for six days and nights. Nevertheless, he recovered sufficiently to construct a ship—a shallow-draught schooner—out of two leaky canoes, with the help of a single soldier. The job took 18 days, and when the schooner was finished the survivors were ready to take to the water.

Before he left, Park sent his Mandingo guide back to the Gambia with his journal and letters. To Sir Joseph he wrote that his new guide, Amadi Fatoumi, 'says that the Niger after it passes Cashna runs directly to the right hand, or the South; yet never heard of any person who had seen its termination.' This information gave the first clear indication of the Niger's southward bend. To his wife he wrote that he was in good health and spirits. 'I think it not unlikely but I shall be in England before you receive this. You may feel sure that I feel happy at turning my face towards home.' And to the Colonial Secretary, he wrote pledging himself to go on to the end. 'Though all the Europeans who are with me should die, and though I were myself half dead, I would still persevere; and if I could not succeed in the object of my journey, I would at least die on the Niger.'

On November 19th, 1805, Park embarked at the riverside town of Sansanding, with one officer, Lieutenant Martyn; three soldiers, one of them half crazy; and three African slaves. The following year rumours of his death reached the Guinea coast; but it was some time before they were substantiated. Then Amadi Fatoumi was traced and gave an outline of the story: he had landed, he said, in order to try and buy provisions and had learned of the tragedy from one of the Africans who had survived. Certain gaps were filled in some years later by other explorers; but even so the full story was not told.

Park had succeeded in reaching the kingdom of Yauri, some 1000 miles below his starting-point and half-way down the eastern side of the enormous arc which the river described. This in itself was a considerable feat of navigation. Unfortunately, however, he had neglected to make friendly overtures to the chiefs through whose territory he had passed, perhaps because he was in a desperate hurry to complete his task while he still had enough strength. Reports of the approach of an infidel white man went before him; and when he reached the rapids at Bussa he was caught in an ambush. It is possible that the schooner struck a rock. It is certain that the boat was attacked and that the crew defended themselves. And then, when the situation had become hopeless, Park and Martyn, one or both of them probably wounded, leapt into the water in an effort to escape from certain death. Both men were drowned.

Park died within 720 miles of his goal. The tragedy is that if only the expedition had started on time, or even if Park had behaved in his normal friendly manner and been more diplomatic in his dealings with the native chiefs, he might well have succeeded. Nevertheless, his achievements were truly remarkable. He was the first European to reach the Niger; he showed that its source must lie somewhere in the eastern slopes of the mountains which form the northern boundary of what is now

Sierra Leone; he navigated the river for more than a thousand miles and gave the first indication of its southward bend. If he never knew the full answer to the problem he had laboured so courageously to solve, he had opened the way for others to find the solution.

V

The Niger Problem Solved

PARK'S BRIEF BUT brilliant career had ended in disaster; and after his death further abortive attempts were made to trace the Niger to its source. In 1815 a three-pronged advance on the river was planned, from Calabar on the Guinea coast, from Morocco, and from Egypt. The plan came to nothing; but in John Lewis Burckhardt, who was earmarked for the Egyptian route, the African Association found a man of great integrity and courage.

Burckhardt, a Swiss who had settled in England and studied Arabic at Cambridge University, was a brilliant scholar. In 1809 he offered his services to Sir Joseph Banks who agreed that he should spend two years in Syria perfecting his Arabic and then travel in the Middle East before attempting the Niger assignment. He hardened himself for the life ahead by sleeping in the open, walking barefoot, and eating nothing but vegetables; for his intention was to pass as a Muslim. 'I am proceeding from hence as an Indian Muhammadan merchant, and shall soon be lost in the crowds of Aleppo,' he informed the African Association in a letter from Malta. He travelled widely, visiting among other places the ancient city of Petra which no European had seen for several hundred years, and arriving in Cairo in 1812. By now his knowledge of Arabic was perfect and, dressed as an Arab, he passed as a learned doctor of Muslim Law. From Cairo he followed the course of the Nile, taking detailed notes on the people and the country, the wild life and ancient monuments. He examined the great temples and the colossal figures of Abu Simbel;* and journeyed as far south as the market town

* They have recently been successfully hoisted from their original positions in order to save them from being submerged by the reservoir formed by the new High Dam at Aswan.

of Shendy, where Bruce had enjoyed a flirtation with the Queen. Then he crossed the Nubian Desert to the port of Suakin on the Red Sea, sailed across to Arabia where, disguised as a Syrian merchant, he made the pilgrimage to the Muslim holy city of Mecca. He may well have become a Muslim (he was buried as one when he died); but if any one had guessed that he was a Christian he would almost certainly have been put to death. Fortunately he aroused no suspicion, and before leaving the area he was able to write a report on the city, the pilgrims and their ceremonies, and the surrounding countryside. Finally, after travelling north to Palestine to visit Mount Sinai, he was ready to begin his search for the sources of the Niger. It was too late: he was in Egypt awaiting the arrival of a caravan to take him into the interior when he died of dysentery. He was only thirty-three.

In 1816 a party of 56 scientists and sailors, led by Captain Tuckey of the Royal Navy, was sent to explore the Congo and find out if it had any connection with the Niger. This expedition also ended in failure and disaster. Many men died from disease: and Tuckey himself died within a few days of reaching the Congo.

While Tuckey's party was on its way to the Congo, two Army officers, Major Peddie and Captain Campbell, set out from the west coast. Peddie died almost at once and Campbell, who got some distance up the Senegal, was forced by sickness to return to the coast. He was succeeded by Captain William Gray who, with Staff-Surgeon Dochard, sailed some distance up the Gambia and then went overland towards the Senegal. They gained the upper waters of the river and Dochard went on ahead to reach the Niger at a point near Segu and not far from Park's embarkation point at Sansanding. He then rejoined the main party; but a further attempt to reach the Niger was thwarted by native chiefs who were afraid the expedition was really in search of gold: and so Gray and Dochard, defeated, retired to the coast.

Three years later—in 1818—a young doctor, Joseph Ritchie,

and a naval officer, George Lyon, arrived in Tripoli. Ritchie had been appointed British Vice-Consul in the Fezzan; but, according to his instructions,

> the grand object of your appointment is the hope that in a little time you may be enabled to proceed under proper protection to Tombuctoo . . . and if you should . . . reach Tombuctoo, you will not fail to collect all possible information as to the further course of the Niger, and of the probability of your being able to trace the stream of that river with safety to its termination or to any given distance towards that point.

Timbuktu, focus of the trading routes from North Africa and the area to the south of the desert, was known to Europeans chiefly through Leo Africanus's description of it as a centre of wealth and culture.

Ritchie and Lyon travelled south from Tripoli to reach Murzuk, capital of the Fezzan. Ritchie died of fever; but although Lyon never got to Timbuktu he amassed a great deal of information about Murzuk and the country lying to the south of it before he was forced to turn back through lack of funds. Like Park before him, Lyon was shocked at the extent of the slave trade. Men and women captured when their villages were raided by Arabs slavers, were bought and sold like cattle, and then marched 1,500 miles to the Mediterranean coast, a ghastly journey which many failed to survive. Lyon joined a slave caravan on his return journey and was sickened by the brutality with which the slaves were treated. 'None of the slave-owners ever marched without their whips, which were in constant use', he noted. One owner 'was so frequently flogging his poor slaves that I was frequently obliged to disarm him'. Whenever a slave gave up and died, he added, the owner 'suspects there must have been something "wrong inside" and regrets not having liberally applied the usual remedy of burning the belly with a red-hot iron.'

While he was in Murzuk, which was itself a slaving centre,

Lyon questioned visiting merchants about Timbuktu and the Niger. The impression he gained was that the legendary city was not nearly as rich and important as Europeans imagined. None of the merchants had actually seen the Niger; but the general opinion seemed to be that it flowed into Lake Chad, in the kingdom of Bornu in central Sudan. Lyon sent this piece of information to London and, as a result, he was ordered to abandon the search for Timbuktu and travel southward to Bornu. These instructions did not reach him: he had already started for home.

Thirty years had now passed since the African Association had sent the first travellers to try and solve the riddle of the Niger. Many brave men had perished: no concrete results had accrued from Park's discoveries, and the riddle remained unsolved. Banks died in 1820, and the Association might have passed under foreign control had it not been for the enthusiasm of Sir John Barrow, patron of Arctic exploration and diplomat, who was Secretary of the Admiralty between 1804 and 1845. Barrow badgered successive British governments into providing funds for further expeditions; and he was instrumental in recruiting the travellers, planning their missions, and safeguarding their interests at home while they were in Africa.

While Barrow was looking around for a suitable replacement for Lyon a twenty-seven-year-old soldier, Major Alexander Gordon Laing, was planning his own assault on Timbuktu. Laing, like Park, was a Scotsman. He was good-looking, slight in build and not over strong, but he was full of self-confidence. He had been a schoolmaster before he decided to join the Army; and his interest in African exploration began when his regiment was stationed in Sierra Leone, which had been founded as a settlement for freed slaves.

Laing's burning ambition was to be the first European to see Timbuktu. He applied for permission and was refused. But in 1821 he was allowed to lead a small party into the interior in search of the sources of the Niger. He was able to determine their position although he did not reach them; and he came to the conclusion—which he could not prove—that there was no possibility of the Niger and the Nile being one and the same river. He was still dreaming of Timbuktu when the following year an expedition was appointed to follow up Lyon's clue that the Niger might flow into Lake Chad.

This expedition was better planned and organized than any of the ill-fated expeditions since the death of Mungo Park. It was led by Walter Oudney, a Scottish doctor of thirty-one, whose chief interests were exploration and natural history. Oudney was a quiet, modest man, physically frail but full of courage. The second member of the party was a fellow Scot, Hugh Clapperton, tall, handsome and exuberant, and two years older than Oudney. At thirteen, Clapperton had gone to sea as a cabin boy in a merchantman. He deserted at Gibraltar, was captured and press-ganged into the Royal Navy to sail the world from the East to the West Indies and Canada. In Canada he hunted with the Red Indians and was accepted as one of themselves; and he had contemplated marriage with a Red Indian princess.

In 1817, however, he was put on half-pay by the Navy and went home to Edinburgh, unemployed. There he met Oudney who lived in the same street, and despite their differences in temperament the two became firm friends.

The third European in the party was Lieutenant Dixon Denham, an Army officer the same age as Clapperton. Denham was arrogant and conceited and a born trouble-maker, very different from the straightforward Oudney, and Clapperton, whom he openly despised. He had met Lyon, who had filled him with some of his own enthusiasm for African exploration; and because he had influential friends at home he had contrived to get himself appointed on equal terms with Oudney and superior to Clapperton.

The party landed at Tripoli early in 1822 and took the desert caravan route to Murzuk. Their further progress was hampered by, among other things, lack of adequate funds; and Denham, ostensibly to smooth out their difficulties but really to try and improve his own standing, departed for London. He returned in due course and was furious to find that, without bothering to ask his permission, Oudney and Clapperton had filled in the time exploring the area between Murzuk and Ghat, to the south. Oudney and Clapperton were equally furious with Denham for deserting his post at a critical moment. The quarrel was patched up; and the expedition joined a caravan bound for Bornu.

Travelling south across the desert the whole party suffered intensely from the merciless heat, violent sandstorms, and a desperate shortage of water. Often when at the end of a wearisome day they reached a well they found it choked with sand and had to spend several hours digging for water and several more before the camels had all been watered. And so they struggled on day after weary day along a route strewn with thousands of human skeletons, a grim reminder of the slaves and their masters who had perished on the desert crossing.

They survived; and once the desert was behind them travelling was easier. They made their way to Bornu; and, on February 4th, 1823, quite suddenly came in sight of their first objective. 'The great Lake Tchad,' wrote Denham, 'glowing with the golden rays of the sun in its strength, appeared to be within a mile of the spot on which we stood. My heart bounded within me at the prospect, for I believed this lake to be the key to the great object of our search. . . .'

Denham, Oudney and Clapperton were the first Europeans to see Lake Chad; but Denham was wrong in thinking that they had found the key to the Niger puzzle. At this stage of the journey he parted from the others and joined a large band of armed Bornuese warriors bound for the mountainous country of Mandara to the south of the lake. Oudney was showing signs of tuberculosis but his courage was high; and he and Clapperton travelled south-east to discover the Shari River and prove that it could not be the Niger. Denham, returning to the lake from what had turned out to be a slave-raiding expedition, was as furious as he had been at Murzuk that the other two had been exploring without him, so furious, in fact, that later on he contrived to suppress Clapperton's account of the expedition.

It was clearly wiser for the party to break up; and so, while Denham explored the Shari and the southern end of the lake, Oudney and Clapperton turned westward in the direction of the Niger, in company with Mohamoud el Wordee, a Muslim merchant from the Fezzan. Their journey took them towards the kingdom of Kano, which had recently been conquered by the Muslim Fulani, a handsome, tawny-skinned people, who had founded their own empire and ruled a population predominantly Hausa. Oudney's professional skill was in great demand. He 'underwent as usual', wrote Clapperton, 'much fatigue—more, indeed, than his strength was equal to: for the news of our arrival spread before us, and at the different towns and villages through which we passed, they brought us all the sick to be cured'.

The strain was too great for Oudney, who died from the tuberculosis against which he had battled so bravely. Clapperton mourned him deeply, as a leader and a friend.

At any time, and in any place, to be bereaved of such a friend had proved a severe trial; but to me, his friend and fellow traveller, labouring also under disease, and now left alone amid a strange people, and proceeding through a country which had hitherto never been trod by European foot, the loss was severe and afflicting in the extreme.

He would not go back, but pressed on and towards the end of January, 1824, he came to the walled city of Kano, capital of the kingdom. He entered the city in some pomp, wearing his naval uniform, expecting to be received with some ceremony. He was, however, 'grievously disappointed; for from the flourishing description of it. . . . I expected to see a city of surprising grandeur: I found, on the contrary, the houses nearly a quarter of a mile from the walls, and in many parts scattered into detached groups, between large stagnant pools of water. I might have spared all the pains I had taken with my toilet', he added ruefully, 'for not an individual turned his head round to gaze at me, but all, intent on their own business, allowed me to pass by without notice or remark.'

Clapperton was aware that Kano was the meeting-place of the Arab caravans from Tripoli and that its slave-market was the focal point. A few days later when he saw the market thronged with crowds 'from all parts of Africa, from the Mediterranean, and the Mountains of the Moon, and from Sennar and Ashantee', he probably understood why the entry of a single naval officer had aroused so little interest. He examined the market with horrified concern. The slaves, carefully decked out for the occasion, were examined by prospective purchasers as though they were animals. Families were ruthlessly broken up; no mother could be sure of keeping her children, no man his wife. Although slaves were often well treated they were doomed to perpetual servitude.

More than half the people of the kingdom of Kano were slaves; and as he travelled through Kano and the kingdom of Sokoto, whose ruler was the head of entire Fulani empire, he found city after city standing empty and deserted, the whole population having been taken as slaves. He therefore approached the Muslim rulers who had received him with every sign of friendship. If they would agree to relinquish the slave trade they could trade with Britain as profitably in legitimate goods, he assured them; but, since Britain herself had by this time renounced the slave trade, the King would not consent to sign a treaty with any ruler who still dealt in slaves.

The rulers agreed to consider the question while Clapperton returned to England to bring it to the attention of the Government. Meanwhile, he asked permission of the chief ruler, Sultan Bello of Sokoto, to proceed to the Niger which, he had been told, was only a few days' march to the west. The Sultan, 'a noble-looking man', clad in a voluminous blue cotton tobe (or shirt), the lower half of his face veiled by the shawl of his white muslin turban, was courteous but adamant: he would not permit the white man to pass on to the river.

And so Clapperton was forced to give up and rejoin Denham, who was waiting at Kuka near Lake Chad. The two men, who could never be friends, recrossed the desert in safety and returned to England together, arriving in London in June, 1825, three and a half years since the date of their departure. Although the expedition had failed in its main task, Lake Chad had been discovered and any possible connection with the Niger disproved. Strange people, new countries, large cities and ancient trade routes had been observed. Geographers need no longer rely on Leo Africanus for their knowledge of the interior of the western part of Africa; for now they were presented with a whole mass of new and important information.

Denham set to work at once on a book, *Narrative of Travels and Discoveries in Northern Nigeria*. In it he inserted Clapperton's description of his journey to Kano and Sokoto; but he did his best to play up his own part in the expedition at the expense of Clapperton and Oudney's, and he did not mention their discovery of the Shari. While Denham was at work on the book Clapperton, broken in health but not in spirit, thought only of returning to Africa to complete his mission.

Alexander Gordon Laing, terrified that Clapperton or some other explorer would beat him in the race to Timbuktu, now redoubled his efforts. While in England on leave he at last got the necessary permission to lead an expedition from Tripoli to Timbuktu and from Timbuktu to trace the course of the Niger to its source. He sailed on February 5th, 1825, taking with him a Negro man servant who had been with him in Sierra Leone and two West African boat-builders, for like Park before him he intended to sail down the river. He was held up for several months in Tripoli, long enough for him to fall in love with Emma Warrington, the beautiful daughter of the British Consul-General, who was himself a great patron of African exploration. The two were married on July 14th; and two days later Laing departed in a small caravan which included an interpreter as well as his servant and the boat-builders. 'I shall do more than has ever been done before,' he boasted, 'and shall show myself to be what I have ever considered myself, a man of enterprise and genius.'

If Laing was arrogant and conceited, very different from the modest Oudney and Clapperton, the man he looked on as his rival, he was also brave and determined. As war had broken out between the local tribes he was forced to make a wide detour; and two months after leaving Tripoli he was still more than a thousand miles from his destination. He was lonely and homesick for his wife; and, from letters which reached him at the village which had sprung up around the oasis of Ghadames, he learned that Clapperton was on the point of landing on the west coast. What he did not know was that a young Frenchman, René Caillié, had also joined in the race to Timbuktu.

Laing set off again, travelling south across the desert, then due west to arrive at the oasis of In Salah in December, 1825. He was the first European to visit In Salah and, as such, he was the object of considerable curiosity. He was invited to appear on the flat roof of the house in which he was staying; and found himself being stared at fixedly by about a hundred women. He was also an object of suspicion. In Salah was crowded with traders from north-western Africa, one of whom was spreading the story that he was really Mungo Park. The man had been wounded in the face by a shot from Park's boat; and persisted in his story, despite the fact that Park's last journey had ended more than twenty years earlier and that Laing was a young man.

Laing concluded that, since Park still had enemies, it would be dangerous for him to try and sail down the river; and, in any event, Timbuktu meant far more to him than the Niger. 'I am not yet in Timbuktu,' he wrote to his father-in-law, 'but I am drawing near to it. . . . I shall not reach the Great Capital before the middle or end of January, but that signifies little. I shall do much more, and render my journey much more interesting, by proceeding quietly and coolly through the country than by

Ripon Falls, Uganda, from a drawing by Captain Grant

Sir Richard Burton, by Lord Leighton

running a race with Clapperton, whose only object seems to be to forestall me in discovery. . . .' At this point Clapperton was in the kingdom of the Yorubas, a kind and friendly people, and about as far to the south of Timbuktu as Laing was to the north. He was making for Kano and Sokoto and not for Timbuktu.

When Laing left In Salah in a large caravan of merchants he hoped that the worst of the journey was over; yet he still had to cross the central part of the desert, a region devoid of large oases and haunted by the fierce nomadic Tuareg tribe. One night while Laing slept the Tuareg attacked the camp, and he was first wounded by a shot and then, when he leapt up to defend himself, terribly slashed with sword thrusts in the head, neck, arms and hands. The merchants had fled at the first signs of trouble; but Laing's interpreter and one of the boat-builders were killed, while the second boat-builder, Laing's camel-driver and servant were all slightly wounded. More dead than alive, Laing was lifted on to a camel, to ride more than 400 miles along the desert route to the headquarters of a friendly sheikh, Sidi Mohammed Muktar, who allowed him to stay in his village while he recovered from his wounds. An epidemic of fever swept the village killing, among others, the Sheikh, Laing's interpreter and the surviving boat-builder. Laing himself caught the fever but recovered; and, after a long delay, persuaded the new Sheikh, who feared for his safety, to let him go on. Before he left, early in August, 1826, Laing wrote a letter to his father-in-law and gave it to the camel-driver who was returning to Tripoli.

I am now the only surviving member of the mission, and my situation is far from agreeable. . . . I have now obtained permission to proceed to Timbuktu but it is at the expense of everything I have got, but I had no alternative, and I consented because I am well aware that if I do not visit it the world will ever remain in ignorance of the place, as I make no vain glorious assertion when I say that it will never be visited by Christian man after me. . . . I am recovering rapidly, but am subject to dreadful pains in my head arising from the severity of my wounds. Love to my dearest Emma, whom may Heaven bless.

The young Sheikh had lent Laing an armed escort; and on August 13th, he arrived in triumph in Timbuktu, after a journey of some 2,650 miles. He was the first European, and the first traveller in modern times, to reach the city by his own efforts.* It was very far from the city of his dreams, a dull, uninspiring place apart from its mosques, with mud houses and no protective walls or natural defences; and its inhabitants—the Songhai people of the Niger—were dominated by the marauding desert Tuareg. But if Laing was disappointed he was not going to admit it. He spent five weeks in the city, apparently wandering about at will, and, despite the obvious danger of a Tuareg attack, he went by night to Kabara, the port of Timbuktu, some five miles distant on the Niger.

Very little is known about how he spent the rest of the time, for only one letter reached the Consul-General at Tripoli.

A very short epistle must serve to apprise you, as well as my dearest Emma, of my arrival at and departure from the great capital of central Africa. . . . I have no time to give you my account of Timbuctoo, but shall briefly state that in every respect except in size (which does not exceed four miles in circumference) it has completely met my expectations. . . .

By this time Laing had given up hope of tracing the Niger upstream to its source. He decided not to return by the fierce desert route but to try and reach Sierra Leone and the west coast; and he joined the caravan of a sheikh who had offered

* There is a strong probability that an American sailor Benjamin Rose (also known as Robert Adams) who was wrecked on the West Coast in 1810, was taken to Timbuktu as a slave and was later released and taken to Morocco to be ransomed by the British Consul and sent to London. Rose told Banks, who interviewed him, that Timbuktu was a miserable place; but opinions differed as to whether he had actually been there or was simply an impostor.

him protection for part of the way. Some thirty miles beyond the city, at a desolate spot called Sahab, the Sheikh and his slaves turned on the infidel Christian and killed him.

Laing had had his moment of triumph and had shown unparalleled courage and daring. He had meant to write a book; but his letters were not informative; his journal disappeared, and so he left behind him very little information about a vast area of unexplored Africa.

By the time Laing was killed, Clapperton had been back in Africa for just over a year. He carried orders from the British Government to 'establish a friendly intercourse' between Britain and Sultan Bello of Sokoto, together with suitable gifts and a letter to the Sultan from King George IV. He was instructed to impress upon the Sultan

the very great advantage he will derive by putting a total stop to the sale of slaves to Christian merchants . . . and by preventing other powers of Africa from marching Koffilas [caravans] of slaves through his dominions. You will inform him of the anxious desire which the King your Master feels for the total abolition of this inhuman and unnatural traffic . . . and that when once the road is open between Raca [Rakah on the Niger] and the sea-coast, he will receive whatever articles of merchandise he may require at a much cheaper rate than he now pays for those which are brought across the long desert.

Clapperton was instructed to collect information on the workings of the slave trade; and

to trace the course of that river which is known with certainty to flow past Kabra [Kabara], or the port of Timbuctoo, & which has been known in modern times by the name of Niger. If this river, contrary to ancient and modern testimonies, should . . . be found to bend its course southward and to fall into the Bight of Benin, instead of continuing to flow to the eastward . . ., and if it should be found to be navigable through the Sultan's territories, or any part thereof, such a discovery may prove of the utmost importance in facilitating the objects of the present Mission and our future intercourse with that Sovereign.

Finally, Clapperton was to find out 'personally if practicable' the sources of the rivers which flowed into the Bights of Benin and Biafra on the Gulf of Guinea and to visit Timbuktu, 'provided you shall not have heard that Major Laing had already accomplished that object'.

Park had given a clear indication of the Niger's southward bend but his report had not been substantiated. Clapperton believed that the Niger flowed into the Bight of Benin and therefore had no connection with Lake Chad. But others, notably Sir John Barrow, were convinced that the Niger would prove to be the Nile.

In November, 1825, Clapperton set out from Badagri on the Bight of Benin on his mission to Sultan Bello. With him were four Europeans, reduced within a few weeks to one—Clapperton's personal servant, a resourceful young Cornishman named Richard Lemon Lander. Also in the party was Pascoe, an elderly man from the Hausa country, who was something of a nuisance on the journey but was to prove the greatest help in times of trouble.

As they passed through the kingdom of the Yorubas they were welcomed everywhere with singing and dancing. At the town of Wawa, not far from Bussa on the Niger, they were pursued by a wealthy widow named Zuma, a buxom woman, so fat that she looked, wrote Lander, 'just like a walking water-butt'. Zuma, who was extremely generous with presents of food and offers of love, first tried her arts on Lander, who 'was but a novice in the art of courtship, and imagining it to be altogether in jest, took little pains to spoil the fun by shrinking from it'. When he realized that she was in earnest the young man gave her 'a flat refusal'; whereupon she transferred her affections to

Clapperton, who extricated himself by leaving the town in a hurry.

Throughout the rest of the journey they were dogged by ill-luck. Clapperton was anxious to learn the truth about Park's death; but at Wawa and at Bussa, where Park was drowned, he found the people very unwilling to talk. By the time they reached Bussa, a town with more than 10,000 inhabitants, both Clapperton and Lander were sick with dysentery; and Clapperton, the first to recover, carried his servant across the streams which the boy was too weak to swim. Just beyond Bussa they crossed the Niger by the Komie ferry; and, having travelled south for some distance, turned north-eastward towards the kingdoms of Zaria and Kano, taking a well-travelled route. Lander was still sick; and at Kano they separated, Lander and Pascoe staying behind with their belongings while Clapperton pressed on alone to Sokoto. When at last he met the Sultan again he found him involved in a war with the ruler of Bornu and far too immersed in military plans to give a thought to trade relations with far-off Britain.

Clapperton had set his heart on carrying out his instructions; and the failure of the mission broke his spirit. Lander, who had made his way from Kano, arrived to find him sick and wretched, growing weaker day by day in the stifling heat.

On Christmas Day, 1826, Clapperton wrote in his journal: 'I gave my servant Richard one sovereign, out of six I have left, as a Christmas gift; for he is well deserving, and has never once shown a want of courage or enterprise unworthy of an Englishman.' Three weeks later he learned of the Tuareg attack on Laing's life but he did not know that Laing had been dead for some months.

By this time he was so weak that he lay all day on a bed which Lander had made for him in the shade outside their hut. 'For five successive days,' wrote Lander, 'I took him in my arms' from the hut to the bed 'and back again at sunset.' After that he was too sick to be moved. During the last weeks of his life Clapperton, who knew he was dying, was torn with a sense of failure and of anxiety about Lander's fate when he himself was dead. Until the very end Lander did everything he could to ease his master's sufferings, nursing and feeding him, fanning him for hours together to cool his burning fever, reading to him daily from the Bible.

When Clapperton realized that the end was near he called the young man to him:

He said, 'Richard, I shall shortly be no more; I feel myself dying.' Almost choked with grief, I replied, 'God forbid, my dear master: you will live many years yet.' 'Don't be so much affected, my dear boy, I entreat you,' said he: 'it is the will of the Almighty; it cannot be helped. . . .'

Clapperton instructed Lander to apply to Sultan Bello for a loan to buy camels and food and to join a caravan bound for the Fezzan. If he was stranded there he should send word to the Consul-General at Tripoli, who would send him what help he needed and make sure that he returned safely to England.

Three days later, on April 13th, 1827, Clapperton died in Lander's arms. The young man solemnly hoisted the Union Jack; and 'then, uncovering my head and opening a prayer-book, amidst showers of tears, I read the impressive funeral service of the Church of England over the remains of my valued master—the English flag waving slowly and mournfully over them at the same moment. . . .'

Clapperton was not quite forty when he died. Although undoubtedly one of the great figures in African discovery, for many years after his death his achievements were underrated. Denham was partly responsible for this neglect. So, too, was Sir John Barrow who, despite all the evidence to the contrary, persisted in his belief that the Niger would prove to be the Nile.

Clapperton had something else to his credit: he had fired his servant with his dedication to the task, thus reinforcing Lander's own splendid qualities, without which he must have despaired. Lander had lost a master who had, as he said, been more like a father to him. He was sick, penniless, the only white man in a vast, almost unexplored region; and his sole companion was Pascoe, the elderly Hausa, who bravely offered to stay with him rather than remain behind in his own country.

Lander was one of the outstanding figures in African exploration. He was born in 1804, the fourth of the six children of a Cornish innkeeper and the grandson of a well-known wrestler. He was short in height and square-looking and, like his grandfather, tremendously strong. His brain was shrewd and keen; his personality charming but direct. Although he had been a servant from the age of eleven, he had always wanted to travel, and he had turned down a much better paid post in order to go to Africa with Clapperton.

He was not going to give up now, even though Clapperton had advised him to go north instead of risking the route to the West Coast: he was far too engrossed with 'the most lively anticipations of solving the geographical problem which had for so long puzzled Europeans, of ascertaining whether the Niger actually joins the sea'. He therefore returned to Kano and then veered southward towards Fundah in the country of Nupe, which he had heard spoken of as a town on the Niger.*

Twelve days' journey from Fundah he was overtaken by a band of armed horsemen sent to arrest him by the Emir of Zaria, ostensibly to protect him from the rulers of Fundah, who were enemies of his overlord the Sultan of Sokoto. Lander, forced to abandon his search, made his way back to Badagri, Pascoe still with him, to await a ship to take him back to England.

It was almost two years since he and Clapperton had landed at Badagri. He found the place swarming with half-caste slave-traders from Brazil, enemies of the British who were endeavouring to break the international slave trade. The traders hinted that Lander was probably a British spy; and they easily convinced the local chief, who lived by slaving, that the young man was a threat to his livelihood.

* Fundah was not, in fact, on the Niger but on its affluent the Benue.

The chief, who countenanced human sacrifice and other cruelties, decided to do away with the intruder. Lander was ordered to appear before the elders

assembled at the fetish hut. . . . On my way five or six hundred people gathered round me, and I could proceed with difficulty. A great number of them were armed with hatchets, bows and arrows, and spears; and waited outside the hut till I came out. On entering one of the men presented me with a bowl, in which was about a quart of liquid much resembling water, commanded me to drink it, saying, 'If you come to do bad, it will kill you, but if not, it cannot hurt you.' There being no resource, I immediately, and without hesitation, swallowed the contents of the bowl, and walked hastily out of the hut, through the armed men, to my own lodgings, took powerful medicine and plenty of warm water, which instantly ejected the whole from my stomach, and I felt no ill effects from the fetish. It had a bitter and disagreeable taste, and I was told it almost always proved fatal.

The chief was so astonished at Lander's survival that he could only think he must be under divine protection and that he himself should provide him with earthly care. He therefore warned Lander that the slave traders were out to murder him and advised him never to go unarmed. For the next two months Lander went in daily fear of his life; but he was rescued by the arrival of a British ship and taken back to England. The faithful Pascoe went all the way to England with him and was then, at his own wish, sent back to his home.

Lander reached home in April, 1828, a year after Clapperton's death. By that time the daring young Frenchman René Caillié, five years his senior, had realized his ambition. Caillié, the son of poor parents, was educated at a charity school and then apprenticed to a trade. He hated the work and took refuge in reading and dreaming. The story of *Robinson Crusoe* (so he wrote in his journal)

inflamed my young imagination; I was impatient to encounter adventures like him; nay, I already felt an ambition
to signalize myself by some important discovery. . . . The
map of Africa, in which I saw scarcely any but countries
marked as desert or unknown, excited my attention more
than any other.

At sixteen Caillié left his trade to go to sea in a ship bound
for Senegal. There he learned that Captain Gray was about to
follow Park's route up the Gambia and he set off on foot to join
the expedition. He reached the Senegal River to find that Gray
had been unable to follow Dochard's lead and that the
expedition was to be abandoned.

In 1824, after returning home sick and disappointed, Caillié
was back on the Senegal. The French Governor of Senegal
provided him with goods and provisions, enough to enable him
to remain while he began to study Arabic 'and the religious
ceremonies of the Moors', so that in due course he would 'be
able to lull their jealous mistrust and thus penetrate the more
easily to the interior of Africa'.

His bold idea was to travel alone in the guise of a devout
Muslim; and he spent three years in Senegal perfecting his
plan. The story he concocted was that he had been born of
Arab parents in Egypt; but that during Napoleon's invasion he
had been taken, as an infant, to France by French sailors. As a
boy he had been a servant, but his master had brought him to
Senegal and given him his freedom. Now, he wished to become a
Muslim and make his way back to Egypt in search of his family.

Caillié's sole disguise was Arab dress, combined with a sound
knowledge of Arabic, of the contents of the Koran and of
Muslim observances. In 1827 he joined a caravan bound for
Timbuktu, thoroughly shaken at the outset by the sight of the
graves of Major Peddie and other members of his ill-fated Niger
expedition. Although his light skin and long nose made him
conspicuous to the tawny-skinned Fulani he lulled their sus-
picions by his obvious piety. But he had to take care never to

be seen writing his journal and, so, cunningly interleaved his copy of the Koran with sheets of blank paper.

Before he reached the left bank of the Niger, Caillié, sick and exhausted, was suffering from a sore foot which refused to heal and had to let the caravan go on without him. For several months he could not move, for his bones were attacked by scurvy. Like Mungo Park before him he owed his life to the kindness of an elderly woman, who fed and nursed him until he was well enough to go on. During his convalescence he 'reflected on the best means of proceeding to the Niger, where I might hope to embark for Timbuktu, the mysterious city which was the object of all my curiosity. . . .'

After walking for two months, still weak and subject to recurring bouts of sickness, he came to an arm of the Niger and was ferried across to the island of Jenne. There he was entertained by some wealthy merchants who, hoodwinked by his disguise, did all they could to help him on his way. Towards the end of March, 1828, he boarded a slave boat bound for Timbuktu. The boat followed the course of the river for some three weeks; and on the morning of April 19th Caillié had his first glimpse of Kabara, the port of Timbuktu. It was just a year since he had joined the caravan at Senegal: during that time he had covered about 1,500 miles, almost 1,000 on foot.

He rode into Timbuktu, eager to see its marvels. The reality was a sad disappointment. The city 'presented at first view, nothing but a mass of ill-looking houses, built of earth. Nothing was seen in all directions but immense plains of quicksand of a yellowish-white colour. . . .' Yet, as he gazed he was filled with admiration for the men who had created a city in the wilderness, and his initial disappointment soon passed.

Protected by his disguise, Caillié was treated as an honoured guest and allowed to go anywhere he wished, to wander about the streets and visit the mosques and the slave-market. The city was 'neither so large nor so populous as I had expected,' he wrote. 'Its commerce is not as considerable as fame has reported. There was not, as at Jenne, a concourse of strangers from all parts of the Sudan. I saw in the streets of Timbuktu only the camels which had arrived from Kabara laden with the merchandise of the flotilla, a few groups of inhabitants sitting on mats conversing together, and Moors lying asleep in the shade before their doors. In a word, everything had a dull appearance. . . .'

Caillié reckoned that the population numbered between 10,000 and 20,000. The people still went in fear of the rapacious Tuareg. He had learned of Laing's death while he was at Jenne; and he could not help dwelling on his fate, especially since he himself had been lent a house near the house where Laing had lodged. He was well aware of his own peril and 'could not repress a feeling of apprehension lest, should I be discovered, I might be doomed to a fate more horrible than death—to slavery'.

Fortunately his disguise was so good that it even deceived the Sheikh of Timbuktu, who received him in audience and questioned him about his treatment in France among the infidel Christians. And so, after spending a fortnight in the city he left, still undetected, to join a caravan bound for Morocco. He thought that if he returned alone to the west coast no one would believe that he had ever been to Timbuktu.

On the journey across 900 miles of desert sandstorms 'wrapped us in darkness like a thick fog', and even the most hardened travellers suffered torments of thirst. It was nearly three months before the caravan entered the Moroccan city of Fez. Still in disguise, Caillié went on to Tangier, where he was smuggled on board a French ship. During the eighteen months of his journey he had covered more than 2,500 miles of largely unexplored territory. He was the first European to visit Timbuktu and return alive to provide, in his *Travels through Central Africa to Timbuctoo*, a first-hand written description. His reward was a small grant from the Geographical Society of Paris, a pension, and a richly deserved Cross of the Legion of Honour. He was forty when he died in 1839.

In the meantime, back home in England Richard Lander had

written an account of his adventures to supplement and complete Clapperton's unfinished Journal; and when this had been published he combined the two histories in a book, *Records of Captain Clapperton's Last Expedition*. He had some help from his younger brother John, who had been apprenticed to a printer and was a compositor on a Cornish newspaper. John Lander, who had himself 'produced several essays in prose and verse', was far more interested in travel than in a career as writer or printer. To his brother, 'there was a charm in the very sound of Africa'; and when Richard Lander asked official permission to try and solve the Niger puzzle John, though quite untried, begged to go with him.

No difficulties were put in their way, and John Lander soon showed that he was an ideal partner.

The brothers sailed from Portsmouth on January 9th, 1830, determined, so Richard wrote to the Colonial Office, 'to condemn every danger and despise every difficulty that may threaten to arrest our progress'. His instructions were to follow the course of the Niger, 'if possible to its termination, wherever that may be', either in the sea or in Lake Chad.

They landed on the west coast, stopping at Cape Coast Castle on their way to Badagri to engage some African servants, among whom was old Pascoe, who brought his two wives along. At Badagri, where the British were thoroughly unpopular and where Richard had narrowly escaped death, they learned that the chief was preparing a human sacrifice of three hundred. They could do nothing to prevent this mass murder; and they were thankful to be able to get away before it began.

They travelled overland towards the Niger by the old route which took them through Yoruba country. The local people were tremendously excited to see them and surrounded the brothers, shouting and squealing, giving them no peace even when they most needed it, when they fell sick with malaria. In Katunga, the capital, however, the King, who could see how much they were suffering, issued an order to Ebo, his chief eunuch, that if any impertinent individual troubles us at any time with his company when it is not desired, Ebo is at liberty to behead him. . . . This proclamation, if it may be so termed, has had the desired effect, for dreading the even-handed Ebo, who is public executioner as well as chief eunuch, the inhabitants of Katunga have hitherto repressed the curiosity, and have confined themselves to their own abodes.

When the brothers reached Bussa they met Richard's old flame, the widow Zuma. The widow, who was fatter than ever, bore Richard no ill-will for spurning her advances, and explained that she had quarrelled with her local chief and was now living in exile.

Richard intended to take to the river at Bussa, but he had great difficulty in securing boats and volunteers to man them. After some delay two canoes were bought in exchange for a quantity of sewing needles, and the brothers embarked on September 20th, 1830. They had absolutely no idea where the windings of the great river would take them nor what dangers and difficulties they might meet on the way.

One of their first problems was the larger of the two canoes, which turned out to be 'extremely leaky and patched in a thousand places'. They used it as long as they could and then abandoned it in favour of a much smaller boat presented to them by a sympathetic chief.

An early encounter, which shook the boatmen's nerve, was with 'an incredible number of hippopotami' which

rose very near us, and came plashing, snorting, and plunging all round the canoe, and placed us in imminent danger. Thinking to frighten them off, we fired a shot or two at them, but the noise only called up from the water, and out of the fens, about as many more of their unwieldy companions, and we were more closely beset than ever.

The terrified boatmen wept aloud, crying that the beasts

would upset the canoes and they would all be drowned; but the brothers, speaking quietly and calmly, urged them to paddle faster until, 'followed by a loud, roaring noise', the canoes shot ahead.

At Egga, the last Nupe town on the Niger, the boatmen threatened to desert. Egga was one of the frontier towns of Hausa: beyond it lay country inhabited by fierce and savage tribes. All save Pascoe and one other man said they could not go further for fear of being killed; but, since it might be equally dangerous for them to remain in Egga, they were at last persuaded to stay with the white men.

A few days later their fears were justified. The party was camping on the river bank just below the confluence of the Niger and the Benue, when

> we beheld a large party of men, almost naked, running in a very irregular manner, and with uncouth gestures towards our little encampment. They were all variously armed with muskets, bows and arrows, knives, cutlasses, barbs, long spears, and other instruments of destruction; . . . Our party was much scattered; but fortunately we could see them coming to us at some distance; and we had time to collect our men. We resolved, however, to prevent bloodshed if possible—our numbers were too few to leave us a chance of escaping by any other way. . . . Not a moment was to be lost. We desired Pascoe and all our people to follow behind us at a short distance with the loaded muskets and pistols; and we enjoined them strictly not to fire, unless they fired first at us. One of the natives, who proved to be the chief, we perceived a little in advance of his companions; and, throwing down our pistols, . . . my brother and I walked very composedly, and unarmed, towards him. As we approached him, we made all the signs and motions we could with our arms, to deter him and his people from firing on us. His quiver was dangling at his side, his bow was bent, and an arrow which was pointed at our breasts, already trembled on the string,

when we were within a few yards of his person. This was a highly critical moment—the next might be our last. But the hand of Providence averted the blow; for just as the chief was about to pull the fatal cord, a man that was nearest him rushed forward and stayed his arm. At that instant we stood before him, and immediately held forth our hands; all of them trembled like aspen leaves; the chief looked up full in our faces, kneeling on the ground—light seemed to flash from his dark rolling eyes—his body was convulsed all over, as though he were enduring the utmost torture, and with a timorous, yet undefinable, expression of countenance, in which all the passions of our nature were strangely blended, he drooped his head, eagerly grasped our proffered hands, and burst into tears. This was a sign of friendship—harmony followed, and war and bloodshed were thought of no more. Peace and friendship now reigned among us; and the first thing that we did was to lift the old chief from the ground, and to convey him to our encampment.

At first they could not understand what the chief was trying to tell them; but then a man appeared who understood the Hausa language and interpreted for him, explaining that the chief, who had never seen white men before, had feared they must be 'Children of Heaven' who had dropped from the skies to take vengeance on him for some past crime. The brothers hastened to assure the old chief that they 'had not come from so good a place as he had imagined [and] congratulated ourselves as well as him that this affair had ended so happily'.

Their act of supreme courage and common sense had undoubtedly saved the lives of the whole party. Before they left the old chief's village they gladly accepted a present of kola nuts and yams, for lack of funds made it impossible for them to buy enough food. Then they set off down the broad Niger. 'Everything was silent and solitary,' they recorded. 'No sound could be distinguished save our own voices and the plashing of the paddles with their echoes; the song of birds was not heard, nor could any animal whatever be seen; the banks seemed to be entirely deserted, and the magnificent Niger to be slumbering in its own grandeur.'

Before long they realized that they must be drawing near the sea. They had reached territory where their white skins no longer made them quite so conspicuous, which meant that it was visited by European traders from the west coast. On November 5th they saw fifty large canoes coming towards them, flying European flags, and manned by Africans in European dress. If they imagined they would get a friendly reception they soon discovered their mistake. The Africans, who were armed, quickly overwhelmed the white men and removed all their belongings, including the jacket and shoes which Richard was wearing. Then

observing some other fellows at the same time taking away Pascoe's wife, I lost all command over myself and was determined to sell my life as dearly as I could. I encouraged my men to arm themselves with their paddles and defend themselves to the last. I instantly seized hold of Pascoe's wife, and with the assistance of another of my men dragged her from the fellow's grasp; Pascoe at the same time levelled a blow at his head with one of our iron-wood paddles that sent him reeling backwards, and we saw him no more.

Fortunately the Africans were not in a warlike mood; but John Lander, who was in the second canoe, was nearly drowned in the fracas.

Courageously—but unwisely—the brothers chased the thieves into the market-place of the nearby river town of Kiri. Instead of regaining their possessions they were captured, their eight followers were put in irons, and they themselves were sent down to the large town of Eboe, where they learned that they and their followers were to be held to ransom, in the expectation that the captain of a British ship which was lying at anchor not far off in the River Nun would pay a good price for them. At

David Livingstone

Henry Morton Stanley, by Herkomer

this point an African merchant, who called himself King Boy, offered to advance the ransom money; and he went off with Richard to find the ship. Very soon Richard, who knew that he was in tidal waters, heard 'the sound of surf on the beach', and realized that the end of his quest was near. Next day—November 18th, 1830—he entered the Nun, the Niger's principal mouth, and saw the British ship. He went on board, to find that four of the crew had just died from fever and that the captain and four more of the crew were sick. To his horror, the captain refused to have anything to do with the transaction, and

made use of the most offensive and shameful oaths I ever heard. 'If you think,' said he, 'that you have a —— fool to deal with, you are mistaken; I'll not give a b——y flint for your bill, I would not give a . . . for it.' Petrified with amazement, and horror struck at such conduct, I shrank from him with terror. I could scarcely believe what I had heard, till my ears were assailed by a repetition of the same. Disappointed beyond measure by such brutal conduct from one of my own countrymen, I could not have believed it possible, my feelings totally overpowered me, and I was ready to sink with grief and shame. . . .

Richard now had to tell King Boy that he could not be paid; and the merchant generously agreed to waive his claim until the money could be sent from England. In due course the British Government honoured the pledge, and King Boy received a sum substantially in excess of the ransom money. In the meantime, the Lander brothers and their followers were taken on board the British ship and carried across to the island of Fernando Po. They returned to England by way of Brazil, arriving in June, 1831.

November 18th, 1830, the day on which Richard Lander first boarded the ship, was a great day in the annals of African discovery. The Landers had traced the course of the Niger to prove conclusively that it emptied itself into the creeks of the

Bight of Benin. The long search was ended: the brothers had triumphantly completed the work of Park, Laing and Clapperton. For his all-important discovery of the Niger mouth Richard Lander was awarded the first Gold Medal of the recently founded Royal Geographical Society, which had absorbed the, by now, moribund African Association. The brothers then wrote up their journals in book form—*Journal of an Expedition to explore the Course and Termination of the Niger*. Despite its pompous title, it is a gay, modest book, entertaining, and packed with valuable material.

The British Government's next move was an attempt to use the Niger as a highway of trade with the interior of West Africa. John Lander, still suffering from the effects of the journey, had taken a job in England, but Richard went as guide to the first trading expedition. From the start everything went wrong. The expedition had scarcely reached the Niger Delta before fever broke out among the white men. The chiefs and their people, who were understandably frightened that their own trade would be ruined, were unfriendly or openly hostile. Richard, however, had the utmost faith in their essential goodness of heart, even when at the Nun mouth they encountered King Jacket, a sullen, ruthless chief. They gave him a present of tobacco and rum, which he grudgingly accepted; but he was overheard to say in his own tongue, 'White man will never reach Eboe this time.'

Richard made light of the threat; but after paddling some 60 miles his canoe was fired on by tribesmen hidden in the undergrowth on the river bank. He was wounded; yet his trust was so strong that he stood up in the boat waving his hat, and attempted, in vain, to convince the boatmen that the shots were merely a form of greeting. His wound was not serious; but it went septic; and the trusting young explorer died. Pascoe, too, died on the river from poison administered by a local chief.

Richard Lander was not quite thirty at the time of his death in 1834. His brother John outlived him by only four years.

VI

Travels in North and West Africa

So MANY LIVES had been lost in the Niger quest that after Richard Lander's death explorers were warned not to take unnecessary risks. There was still exploratory work to be done in the area of the river and in the regions bordering on the Sahara. The three outstanding explorers of the second half of the nineteenth century were two Germans, the scientist Heinrich Barth, and Gerhard Rohlfs, who started his African career in the French Foreign Legion; and a Frenchman, Louis-Gustave Binger.

Heinrich Barth, who was born in Hamburg in 1821, completed his studies at Berlin University and then visited Africa for the first time. In 1849 he joined a British-sponsored expedition to explore the southern Sahara and visit its Muslim kingdoms. It was led by an Englishman, James Richardson, and the third European was a German, Ludwig Overweg.

Barth, a young man of considerable learning, had a gift for languages. He understood English and Arabic and had no difficulty in mastering the tongues of various African peoples. He had already travelled in lesser-known parts of Syria and Asia Minor; and it was his craving for knowledge rather than his craving for adventure that led him to join the Richardson expedition. He was, however, tremendously strong and resilient; and when it came to the point he was to prove himself both courageous and resourceful.

James Richardson was over forty, much older than Barth and Overweg, who was twenty-six. Richardson, a serious man destined originally for the Church, had landed at Tripoli in

1845 under the aegis of a Bible society and travelled south to Murzuk, with the combined objectives of fostering Christianity and trying to substitute trade in legitimate goods for the slave trade. His approach to exploration was as cautious as the Government could wish:

> I am very much of the opinion that in African travel we should take especial care not to attempt too much at once, that we should proceed very slowly, feeling our way, securing ourselves against surprise, and reducing and confining our explorations to the record of matters of fact as far as possible. ... African travel can only be successfully prosecuted piecemeal, bit by bit, here a little and there a little, now an island, now a line of coast, now an inland province, now a patch of desert.

Such caution was foreign to the energetic Barth, who always wanted to be up and away. Leaving Tripoli early in 1850, the party crossed the desert and in a month had reached Murzuk. They planned to continue southward through Ghat and Agades to the kingdoms of Kano and Bornu; and they had nearly reached Ghat, which Oudney and Clapperton had visited in 1822, when Barth, restless and impatient, went off by himself to climb a high cliff. Despite his self-confidence he lost himself in the sandy wastes of the desert; and he was alone for over twenty-four hours, suffering such agonies of thirst that he opened a vein and drank some of his own blood. He would undoubtedly have perished if he had not been found by a solitary Tuareg, who humanely carried him back to camp on his camel. 'Twenty eight hours without water in the desert!' exclaimed Richardson. 'Our people could scarcely at first credit that he was alive: for their saying is that no one can live more than twelve hours when lost in the desert during the heats of the summer. . . .'

Barth had learnt his lesson. 'It is, indeed, very remarkable,' he wrote, 'how quickly the strength of a European is broken in these climes, if, for a single day, he is prevented from taking his usual food. Nevertheless,' he added with pardonable pride, 'I was able to proceed the next day.'

They spent a week in Ghat; but not long after they left they were captured by a band of Tuareg, who took a third of all their supplies and belongings before setting them free. The party then split up: Barth was to go on to Kano; Richardson to the town of Zinder, due north of Kano but nominally in the kingdom of Bornu; and Overweg to Lake Chad. They arranged to rendezvous at Kuka, near Lake Chad. 'We took leave of one another with some emotion,' wrote Richardson sombrely, 'for in Central Africa those travellers who part and take divergent routes can scarcely count on all meeting again.'

Richardson was the only one who failed to arrive at the meeting-place. He reached Zinder on January 4th, 1851, and was appalled by the barbarous customs countenanced by the local sultan, particularly by the treatment of slaves. The sultan, self-appointed executioner, killed his victims by slitting open their chests and tearing out their hearts. Executions went on continuously; and in this doom-laden atmosphere Richardson sickened and died.

Barth, meanwhile, had arrived in the city of Kano. He was almost destitute, but his friendly disposition and knowledge of languages appealed to the Emir. When he had finished his inspection of the city the Emir made him a present of 60,000 cowries (the currency used in the area), and with this money Barth was able to buy camels to carry him on to Bornu, where he intended to investigate the kingdom's trade. The journey was full of hazards. 'There was no caravan,' wrote Barth; 'the road was infested by robbers; and I had only one servant upon whom I could rely, or who was really attached to me, while I had been so unwell the preceding day as to be unable to rise from my couch. However, I was full of confidence. . . .'

He reached Kuka a month ahead of Overweg and, when he learned of Richardson's death, took charge of the expedition and carried out an examination of Lake Chad. The character of the lake, he wrote, is evidently that of an immense lagoon, changing its border every month, and therefore incapable of being mapped with accuracy. Indeed, when I saw to-day [April 24th, 1851] the nature of these swampy lowlands surrounding the lake or lagoon I immediately became aware that it would be quite impossible to survey its shores even if the state of the countries around should allow us to enter upon such an undertaking...

He was becoming increasingly worried about Overweg, who was sick and depressed and showed signs of mental derange-ment. But the young man refused to give up, and together they turned southward to Yola, chief city of the province of Adam-awa. They were making for the upper waters of the Benue, the Niger's greatest tributary, which until that time had been known only in its lower reaches. At Yola Barth found that

the Benue flowed . . . from east to west, in a broad, majestic course, through an entirely open country, from which only here and there detached mountains stand forth. . . . I had now, with my own eyes, clearly established the direction and nature of this mighty river. . . . I looked long and silently upon the stream; it was one of the happiest moments of my life.

The discovery of the upper Benue was probably Barth's chief contribution to geographical knowledge. He was anxious to push farther south but the governor of Yola refused to let him go on. He therefore retraced his route to Kuka, and took a trip to the north of Lake Chad. Then, leaving Overweg to continue the examination of the lake, he set out to try and reach 'the regions south of Baghirmi'. He struck the Shari at Bougoman, noting everything he saw with painstaking thoroughness, delv-ing into the history of the city as well as its present conditions, remarking that its ruler had to pay a yearly tribute of a hundred slaves to his overlord, the Sultan of Bornu. He then returned to Kuka, where he found poor Overweg sick and raving mad.

Overweg died soon afterwards, leaving Barth, now the sole European survivor, completely destitute.

Barth took his companion's death philosophically and with detachment. 'I determined to set out as soon as possible on my journey toward the Niger,' he declared, 'to new countries and new people.' He was not 'discouraged after the death of my comrade Overweg', he wrote in a letter home. 'I find my powers redoubled. I feel as strong as a giant.' He was intoxicated by the possibility of 'succeeding in the field of the glorious career of Mungo Park', the one explorer for whom he had unstinted admiration.

At this juncture despatches arrived from England with money and instructions to proceed at once to Timbuktu. Barth travelled by way of Sokoto and Say, on the Niger. At Sokoto he was received by the Sultan, to whom he gave a number of gifts, including a pair of richly mounted pistols, a red satin cloak lined with yellow, red cloth trousers, three turbans, two pairs of razors, and half a dozen looking-glasses. The Sultan, a son of Sultan Bello whose refusal to consider a trading treaty with Britain had broken Clapperton's heart, 'expressed, in a very feeling way, his regret' at the incident.

Barth approached Timbuktu by the route followed 'by that very meritorious French traveller, René Caillié'; and, like Caillié, he wore Arab dress, though much against his conscience. But, while Caillié had taken the greatest care to preserve his disguise, Barth relied on the protection of the powerful and friendly Sheikh el Bakay. When, however, sick and weary, he entered the city he found to his dismay that the Sheikh was not there. One of the Sheikh's enemies, learning that a Christian infidel had entered the city, spread a rumour that he was really Laing's son: and the son of Laing's murderer now swore to kill Barth. At the moment of crisis this man died suddenly and mysteriously. His death was received by his fellow conspirators as a sign of divine intervention, an indication that Barth must not be harmed. The providential return of Sheikh el Bakay gave him an opportunity of studying the city slowly

and thoroughly. While confirming 'the general accuracy' of
Caillié's account of his journey, he commented sourly on 'the
great inaccuracy which characterizes' his view of the town.
Barth was always a fault-finder; and, Mungo Park apart, he
was quick to criticize his predecessors for inaccurate observation. On this occasion, he conceded that

> on the whole, the character of the single dwellings was well
> represented by that traveller, the only error being that in his
> representation the whole town seems to consist of scattered
> and quite isolated houses, while, in reality, the streets are
> entirely shut in, as the dwellings form continuous and
> uninterrupted rows.

Barth's survival—and the fact that he was able to spend as
long as eight months in Timbuktu—was really due to his
learning and his capacity for friendship. El Bakay was delighted
to meet a European who could read the Koran and discuss
Muslim observances with him. Barth himself wrote that 'I have
never proceeded onward without leaving a sincere friend behind
me, and thus being sure that, if obliged to retrace my steps, I
might do so with safety.'

After leaving Timbuktu, Barth sailed down the Niger to Say
and then travelled overland through Sokoto and Kano towards
Bornu. He still had an assortment of suitable gifts; and at each
stopping-place he presented a looking-glass to the most handsome woman, 'the rest receiving nothing but needles'. Once,
when asked to show himself in European clothes, he produced
from his baggage a black dress suit which created a 'rather un-
favourable idea of our style of clothing'.

He had learned already that another British-sponsored
expedition was on its way to central Africa, led by a young
German scholar, Dr Edward Vogel. Not long after leaving
Kano,

> I saw advancing towards me a person of strange aspect; a
> young man of very fair complexion, dressed in a robe like the

one I wore myself, and with a white turban wound thickly round his head. He was accompanied by two or three blacks, likewise on horseback.

One of the Africans, a former servant of Barth's, told the young man who he was, 'in consequence of which Mr Vogel (for he it was) rushed forward and, taken by surprise as both of us were, we gave each other a hearty reception from horseback.'

Barth learned with annoyance that Vogel, believing him to be dead, had sent home a report to that effect; and so he decided to return himself to break the news of his survival. The two men parted, Vogel to complete Barth's exploration to the south of Lake Chad and to explore the territory between the lake and the Nile. On his journey across Africa Vogel reached Wadai, about a third of the distance to the Nile, and there he was murdered. No fewer than seven expeditions were sent out to find him. Only one, under another German, Maurice von Beurmann, succeeded in reaching Wadai; and in 1863 Beurmann, too, was murdered.

Barth, meanwhile, had crossed the desert to Murzuk and Tripoli and had arrived in England in the autumn of 1855, after a journey lasting more than five years. It was a record of heroic endurance and it yielded great geographical results. And yet, although Barth was awarded the Patron's Medal of the Royal Geographical Society in 1865, his discoveries were not immediately followed up. He remained unknown to the general public, whose interest and attention had by this time been drawn to important discoveries in southern Africa. In his book, *Travels and Discoveries in North and Central Africa, 1849–55*, he explained the tremendous scope of his work.

Extending over a tract of country of twenty-four degrees from north to south, and twenty degrees from east to west, in the broadest part of the continent of Africa, my travels necessarily comprise subjects of great interest and diversity. After having traversed vast deserts of the most barren soil,

and scenes of the most frightful desolation, I met with fertile
lands irrigated by large navigable rivers and extensive central
lakes, ornamented with the finest timber, and producing
various species of grain, rice, sesamum, ground-nuts, in
unlimited abundance, the sugar cane, etc., together with
cotton and indigo, the most valuable commodities of trade.
The whole of Central Africa, from Baghirmi to the east as far
as Timbuktu to the west, . . . abounds in these products. The
natives of these regions not only weave their own cotton, but
dye their home-made shirts with their own indigo. The river,
the far-famed Niger, which gives access to these regions by
means of its eastern branch, the Benue, which I discovered,
affords an uninterrupted navigable sheet of water for more
than six hundred miles into the very heart of the country.
Its western branch is obstructed by rapids at a distance of
about three hundred and fifty miles from the coast; but even
at this point it is probably not impassable in the present state
of navigation, while, higher up, the river opens an immense
highroad for nearly one thousand miles into the very heart of
Western Africa, so rich in every kind of produce.

Although well aware of the importance of his achievements
Barth was far from boastful. Of his journey to Timbuktu and
his exploration of parts of the Niger,

which, through the untimely fate of Mungo Park, had
remained unknown to the scientific world, I succeeded to my
utmost expectation and not only made known the whole of
that vast region which, even to the Arab merchants in
general, had remained more unknown than any other part
of Africa, but I succeeded also in establishing friendly relations with all the most powerful chiefs along the river up to
that mysterious city itself. . . . No doubt even in the track
which I myself pursued, I have left a good deal for my
successors in this career to improve upon; but I have the
satisfaction to feel that I have opened to the view of

the scientific public of Europe a most extensive tract of the secluded African world, and not only made it tolerably known, but rendered the opening of a regular intercourse between Europeans and these regions possible.

Barth returned to Germany after the publication of his book. In 1863 he was made Professor of Geography; but until his death two years later at the age of forty-four he continued to travel as often as possible in the Middle East.

It was some time before the real worth of his discoveries was appreciated: but in 1890 another explorer, Joseph Thomson, aptly described Barth's work in his book *Mungo Park and the Niger*. 'Never before,' wrote Thomson, 'had such a rich harvest of geographical, ethnographical, and philological facts been gathered in the African field of research.'

Many years earlier, in 1854, following Vogel's report of Barth's death, a search party was sent to Africa led by a Naval surgeon, William Balfour Baikie. The expedition failed to make contact with Barth: but it proved that the Niger and—to some extent—the Benue were navigable to steamships. Even more significant, it proved the value of quinine as a preventive to the dreaded malaria; for on a 300-mile voyage up the Benue not a single member of the party died from fever.

Vast areas of hitherto unknown northern Africa were explored by the German Gerhard Rohlfs, who began his African career in 1855 when, at the age of 23, he joined the French Foreign Legion in Algeria as an apothecary's assistant. He was involved in the French campaign of 1857 which resulted in the conquest of Kabylie; and five years later he set out on his wanderings, starting from Tangier disguised as a Muslim physician.

For the next 16 years Rohlfs travelled extensively. He visited Fez and Morocco and followed the north-west coast down to Wady Sus before turning inland to Tafilet, which Caillié had visited on his return journey from Timbuktu. In 1863 he tried, but failed, to cross the desert to Timbuktu; but the following year, after visiting Tafilet for the second time, he travelled south-east to become the first European to visit the oasis of Tuat. He made the return journey to Tripoli by way of the oasis of Ghadames, where Laing had been detained on his journey to Timbuktu. In 1865 he crossed the desert from Tripoli, proceeding to Bornu and on to the Benue, down which he sailed to its confluence with the Niger.

A few years later—in 1869—another German, G. Nachtigal, was in the same vast area. Starting from Tripoli, Nachtigal penetrated the eastern Sahara as far as Tibesti, found a new route to Kuka, and explored the regions to the north and south-east of Lake Chad; and then, instead of recrossing the desert to Tripoli, returned to Cairo by way of Wadai, where Vogel had been killed; Darfur; and the province of Kordofan.

In 1874, after two years spent wandering in Ethiopia, Rohlfs led an expedition across the Libyan Desert to the oasis of Siwa, a march which took a little over a month. In 1878 he was again in Tripoli, planning to get to Wadai: he failed, getting only as far as the oasis of Kufra. This was the last of his main journeys, for which he had already been awarded the Patron's Medal of the Royal Geographical Society. In 1885, at the age of 53, he started a new career as German Consul at Zanzibar. He died in 1896.

The third of the major explorers—Louis-Gustave Binger—was born in 1856 and lived to a ripe old age, dying in 1937. Binger, a soldier, first came to Africa on military service. His subsequent journeys were undertaken with the object of determining international boundary lines; but he himself was as interested in geographical discovery as in the annexation of territory by France. His first and most important journey, which lasted from 1887 to 1891, took him into undiscovered country to the south of the Niger bend. It had been generally believed hitherto that the valley of the Niger was very wide; but Binger proved, on the contrary, that it was quite narrow. He also proved that the Volta River rose near the course of the Niger: and he was able to disprove the existence of a large mountain range shown on a number of existing maps as straddling the country at about latitude 10° North.

Binger was awarded the Founder's Medal of the Royal Geographical Society for his discoveries. Later, in 1892, he penetrated more than 1,200 miles into largely unknown country with the object of determining the boundary line between the British Gold Coast (now Ghana) and the French Ivory Coast; and he was appointed Governor of the Ivory Coast in 1893.

Binger's work was supplemented by others, notably by the Frenchman P. L. Monteil. Starting from Senegal in 1892, Monteil crossed the Niger bend at Say, travelled to Lake Chad by way of Sokoto and Bornu, and then crossed the desert from Lake Chad to Tripoli.

There was still work to be done; but by this time the era of exploration had given way to the international 'Scramble' for Africa between Britain and the major European Powers.

VII

Explorer-Missionaries in Southern and Eastern Africa

IN 120 YEARS, between 1768 when James Bruce set out on his travels and 1888, East and Central Africa were made known to the outside world. Penetration of the eastern side of the continent proceeded from many points at once. Some pioneers started from the north, up the Nile Valley, or from the Red Sea ports through Somaliland; some thrust inland from the island of Zanzibar off the east coast, making for the great lakes of Central Africa; others reached the same area from the south.

Before continuing the main exploration story it is necessary to take a look at the penetration of the southern part of the continent. As we saw, the disappearance of the Portuguese coastal settlements in the sixteenth century was followed during the latter part of the seventeenth by the arrival in the Cape of the Dutch. The native population of the Cape, scattered and few in numbers, were Bushmen and Hottentots, unwarlike peoples. The Bushmen fled into desert country; the majority of the Hottentots were enslaved by the Dutch. The settlers were discouraged by the Dutch East India Company from developing a colony and for a time the European population of the Cape remained small; but the Company was powerless to prevent individual settlers from penetrating farther and farther inland. In the interior the settlers encountered Bantu-speaking tribes who were spreading southward from Central Africa in search of new pasture lands. Some of these people were quiet and peaceable: others, fierce and warlike, preyed on the weaker tribes and clashed with the settlers.

Despite these difficulties exploration continued: and by the end of the eighteenth century the country was known in broad outline up to the Orange River and at some points in the west beyond it into South West Africa.

In Europe, the Napoleonic Wars had broken out in 1795, and the British occupied the Cape to protect the sea route to India, retaining it at the Peace Treaty of 1814. The Afrikaaners (or Boers as they were generally called), the descendants of the original settlers and mainly of Dutch extraction, resented British interference and control, and many of them began to trek away. The subsequent history of South Africa was of conflict between British and Afrikaaner and of a clash between two invasions—one European, one Bantu—sweeping in from opposite directions.

Friction between British and Afrikaaner culminated in 1833. In that year Britain passed the Abolition of Slavery Act which set free all the slaves in the British Empire, including Cape Colony, and allocated the sum of £20 million as a free gift to compensate the slave owners for their loss, a sum which represented very much more than its present-day value implies. The Afrikaaners were, of course, granted compensation for the loss of their slave labour; but payment was made in London and, since the slave-owners could not go to England to collect, the money had to pass through the hands of agents. The agents were rapacious and unscrupulous; and such compensation as reached the slave-owners was almost non-existent. The freed slaves, who were obliged to work for their former owners as apprentices for five years, stayed on permanently when they could; but many of them, unwanted by masters who could not—or would not—pay them, were simply left to their fate.

The emancipation of the slaves was one of the chief reasons why the bulk of the Afrikaaners left the Cape in the Great Trek of 1836. They fought desperate battles with the Zulu and other warlike tribes; but within a few years they had occupied vast areas of land, reaching as far north as the Limpopo River. In

1852 they founded the Transvaal and two years later the Orange Free State.

The outlines of this huge area were explored by the great explorer-missionary David Livingstone. Born in 1813 in Scotland, of poor, deeply religious parents, Livingstone started work in a cotton factory at the age of ten and attended night school when the day's work was done. His ambition was to become a medical missionary; and by the age of twenty-three he had saved up enough money to pay his fees at a medical school. On the advice of a famous missionary, Dr Robert Moffat, who had worked for many years for the London Missionary Society in South Africa, Livingstone, too, chose Africa. He was fired by the older man's suggestion that he 'would do for Africa' if he was 'prepared to leave occupied ground and push on to the North'.

Livingstone arrived in South Africa in 1841. He was twenty-eight years old, strongly built, ungainly in movement, and slow in speech, with a blunt, direct manner, and an over-powering sense of duty. From Cape Town he journeyed over five hundred miles by ox wagon to Moffat's mission settlement at Kuruman. Once there he started to study the Sechuana and other related African languages and learn all he could of the history and customs of the people among whom he was to live. There, too, he met and married Moffat's daughter Mary, 'not romantic, but a matter-of-fact lady, a little thick, black-haired girl, sturdy and all I want'. Mary Moffat was the ideal wife for a man who believed that a pioneer missionary must be much more than 'a man going about with a Bible under his arm'. There was no hardship she was not prepared to face at his side; and she could, and did, endure years of enforced separation without complaint. And when her husband thought it wise to take her and their three young children across the dreaded Kalahari Desert she accompanied him without a moment's hesitation.

Within two years of his arrival Livingstone was building his own mission-house at Mabotsa, two hundred miles to the north-east of Kuruman; and it was at Mabotsa that he very nearly lost his life. A man-eating lion, one of a pride which had been terrorizing the native village, 'caught me by the shoulder and we both came down together. Growling horribly he shook me as a terrier dog shakes a rat. It caused a sort of dreaminess in which there was no sense of pain or feeling of terror, though I was conscious of all that happened.' The lion, which had already been wounded, was dispatched by an African armed with a spear. Livingstone was badly mauled: his wounds were slow to heal and for the rest of his life he could not move his left arm and shoulder without acute pain. When, however, he was asked his impressions of the incident, he remarked laconically, 'I was wondering which part of me he would eat first.'

Livingstone's pioneering instincts were too strong to allow him to stay in one place for long; and after four years at Mabotsa he pushed on towards the north and established himself at Kobolong on the eastern edge of the Kalahari Desert. There he stayed for five years, the only real period of home life he and his wife ever enjoyed. Then he joined two friends, European big-game hunters, and crossed the desolate wastes of the desert to become the first white men to set eyes on Lake Ngami, 870 miles north of Kuruman. Two years later Livingstone again crossed the desert, hoping to find a suitable site near the lake for a mission-station. His wife and children accompanied him, and they all nearly died of thirst.

By this time Livingstone had conceived the idea of discovering a great waterway which would carry boats from the interior of Africa to the sea and would bring missionaries and traders from the coast. But if Christianity was to flourish in the interior he must first find a 'salubrious climate' for new mission-stations. To his disappointment Lake Ngami was unhealthy and fever-ridden: and so he pushed on far beyond the lake to the banks of 'a glorious river', the Zambezi. Here was the very heart of Africa, where white men were unknown.

Livingstone had reached the Zambezi by way of Linyanti, home of the Makololo, whom he admired above all the other Bantu tribes and over whom he gained considerable influence.

'We like you as well as if you had been born among us,' they told him. 'You are the only white man we can become familiar with; but we wish you would give up that everlasting preaching and praying. You see we never get rain, while tribes who never pray as we do obtain it in abundance.' Livingstone's reply was to give his Makololo friends a lesson in 'leading out their river for irrigation'.

In the course of his journey he had seen ghastly evidence of the ravages of the Arab slave trade and of the internal tribal trade. The Arabs were pushing deeper and deeper into the interior, depopulating and devastating large areas of country. Torn with indignation and with pity for the unfortunate slaves, he set himself to cleanse 'this open sore of the world'. He believed that this could be done only by opening the country to Christianity and legitimate trade. To this end he decided on an investigation which would take him across the continent to the west coast. In 1852, having taken his family to Cape Town en route for England, he trekked north to Linyanti, where he recruited 27 Makololo porters. In November, 1853, he set off down the Chobe River and into the Zambezi; and within seven months, travelling partly by canoe but mostly on foot, he reached the Portuguese port of Loanda, a journey of some 1,500 miles. He was weakened by repeated attacks of fever, and had had great difficulty in coaxing the Makololo through country infested with hostile tribes, but their devotion to him had triumphed over their very natural fears.

At Loanda he was offered a passage to England on a British ship. He refused: he intended to cross Africa from west to east and to see his followers safely home. The return journey to Linyanti took a year; but after a few weeks' rest he set off for the east coast. A short trip down the Zambezi brought him in sight of some magnificent waterfalls. The river, at this point nearly a mile broad, disappeared with a roar into a narrow fissure hundreds of feet below. Thence it churned and boiled in its course for miles along a deep gorge, flinging up columns of vapour. The Makololo called these waterfalls 'the smoke that thunders': Livingstone, the first white man to see them, named them the Victoria Falls, after the Queen.

For a time he followed the course of the river, hoping to find it navigable from the falls to the east coast, thus giving easy access to the interior. Leaving the course of the river for a while, he struck north-east in an unsuccessful search for 'healthy ridges' for mission-stations. Then he turned again towards the coast and reached Tete, a Portuguese settlement some 250 miles inland.

After arranging for his Makolo followers to await his return from England, he sailed down the river to the seaport of Quilimane at the northern end of the Zambezi delta.

In his passage across Africa—one of the finest achievements in the whole history of exploration—Livingstone had covered 6,000 miles. The observations he had taken on a journey which had lasted just under four years were so accurate that years later the Astronomer Royal could write:

> What that man has done is unprecedented. . . . You could go to any point across the entire continent along Livingstone's track and feel certain of your position. His are the finest specimens of geographical observation I have ever met with.

From Quilimane Livingstone sailed for home, eager to see his wife and children again. He had left England fifteen years earlier, unknown and untried: he returned to find himself a national hero. Success did not change him. 'After eighteen months of laudation,' wrote Sir Roderick Murchison, Chairman of the Royal Geographical Society, 'and after receiving all the honours which the universities and cities could shower on him, he is still the same honest, true-hearted David Livingstone as when he issued from the wilds of Africa.'

During his period at home Livingstone wrote the first of his three books, *Missionary Travels*. Like the others, *The Zambesi and its Tributaries*, and *Last Journals*, which was edited and published after his death, it is packed with invaluable scientific and geographical information and lively descriptions of Africa and the people he loved so well.

Before leaving for Africa again in 1858 he made a passionate pleas for young missionaries to follow him in his endeavour 'to make an open path for commerce and Christianity.' He returned under Government aegis, as British Consul at Quilimane, with instructions to explore the Zambezi valley and examine the possibilities of using it as a trading highway. This time he brought European assistants with him, among them his brother and a young doctor and botanist named John Kirk, who was later to play a vital part in the suppression of the Arab slave trade.

The five years of the Zambezi expedition were among the most exacting, and certainly the most troubled, of Livingstone's life, although at the outset everything seemed set fair. At Tete, the expedition's base, he received a rapturous welcome from his Makololo followers. 'The men rushed into the water up to their necks in their eagerness to see their white father,' wrote one of Livingstone's assistants. 'Their joy was perfectly frantic. They seized the boat and nearly upset it and carried the Doctor ashore singing all the time that their Father was alive again.' In the course of the expedition Livingstone kept his promise to lead the Makololo back to their tribe; but there were moments when he wished most fervently that he could have kept them with him.

His troubles soon began. He found the Portuguese officials friendly; but before long he found out that many of them were profitably engaged in the slave trade, and when he realized this he was ruthlessly outspoken in his condemnation. He was outspoken, too, with his assistants from whom he demanded unquestioning obedience, with powers of endurance and a disregard for sickness as strong as his own. 'An unfortunate expedition for quarrels,' was Kirk's verdict; for often there was friction between the leader and his followers, and his own brother was a prime mischief-maker. Of the entire party Kirk was the only man to approach Livingstone in quality; yet, despite his devotion to the older man, he was well aware of his failings. He knew that the years of loneliness, strain and fever had taken a heavy toll of Livingstone's temper as well as his strength, and that the Doctor, who was happy and at ease with all Africans, could be stiff or impatient with Europeans and was sometimes moody and distracted. For Livingstone an overwhelming sorrow was his wife's death from fever in 1862. She had come out to join him; and her death, a personal disaster for Livingstone, was a blow to the whole party, for her sane and soothing influence might have smoothed out the differences between them.

It was a bitter disappointment to Livingstone to discover that the Zambezi was unnavigable for long stretches and could never serve as a highway into the interior. Nevertheless the expedition achieved some considerable results. Livingstone and Kirk were the first Europeans to set foot in the country of Nyasaland (now Malawi). They discovered Lake Shirwa, and reached Lake Nyasa, one of the largest of Africa's inland seas; and the discovery at length of healthy uplands, the Shire Highlands, gave Livingstone intense satisfaction, for 'in this new region no end of good could be effected in developing the trade in cotton and discouraging that in slaves'.

Everywhere they went Livingstone and Kirk found fresh and appalling instances of slave raiding. Near Lake Nyasa thousands of starving, homeless Africans were fleeing from the stronger tribes who captured and sold them to the Arab slavers. No fewer than 19,000 slaves from Nyasaland alone were shipped yearly from the port of Zanzibar across the Indian Ocean. Livingstone reckoned that only a tenth of those captured reached the east coast alive; and the shores of the lake were strewn with the bones of the dead. His book, *The Zambesi and its Tributaries*, contained such a terrible indictment of the slave trade that a Select Committee of the British House of Commons recommended that whatever the cost, even if it meant the annexation of Zanzibar and the adjoining mainland, slavery in East Africa must be abolished.

Livingstone was not, of course, the only man to appeal for the establishment in Africa of Christian missions. During the first half of the nineteenth century, as the Afrikaaners in South Africa began to trek away from British interference, missionaries were pushing their way inland. Their primary object was not exploration, but there were some remarkable travellers among them.

The East African story opens with the travels of an intrepid pair of Germans, Johann Ludwig Krapf and Johann Rebmann. Krapf, the son of a farmer, was born in Württemberg in 1810. He was a delicate child, nervous, introspective and studious, much given to reading the Bible. His interest in travel was awakened when he read Bruce's *Travels to Discover the Source of the Nile*. 'Is there then so great a desert yonder . . . untrodden by the foot of any European?' he mused as he studied the map of eastern Africa. He was still musing over this astonishing fact when a missionary lectured at his school on the work of the overseas missions. In a flash young Krapf knew what he wanted to do: he would be a man of God and he would preach the Gospel in Ethiopia where Bruce had been before him. He left school to train in a missionary college in Basle and then joined a branch of the Church Missionary Society in Adowa in northern Ethiopia. After a short stay in Adowa he moved farther south to preach to the pagan tribes of Shoa. He was much drawn to the Galla tribes and thought, mistakenly, that they occupied a large part of Central Africa and that a mission to them would be of the utmost importance. The Galla, he noted, were a proud, intelligent people, powerfully built and skilled horsemen. 'Even the women gallop beside or behind their husbands,' he wrote, 'for among them it is considered degrading to go on foot.'

Krapf pursued his mission with diligence and zeal: but the local chiefs were hostile and in 1843 he was expelled from the country. He left Ethiopia with his wife, a German girl whom he had married the previous year, with instructions to go to Zanzibar and, from there, to prospect on the adjoining mainland for a suitable site for a mission-station. On the way his wife gave birth to a baby girl who did not survive the journey. The Krapfs were hospitably received by the small European community of Zanzibar and Krapf was presented to the Sultan, descendant of an Arab dynasty grown rich on the profits of the slave trade which had pushed its authority deep into the hinterland of East Africa. The Sultan was perfectly willing for Krapf to proceed, and dictated for him a form of passport: 'This comes from Said-Said Sultan: greetings all our subjects, friends, and governors. This letter is written in behalf of Dr Krapf, the German, a good man who wishes to convert the world to God. Behave well to him, and be everywhere serviceable to him.'

This passport proved effective among the Nyika and Kamba tribes of the mainland; and the Krapfs settled down at Mombasa, Krapf to proselytize the pagan tribes and study Swahili and other African languages. He dreamed of establishing a chain of mission-stations right across the continent, from east to west.

Mombasa was an unhealthy place. Krapf's wife and a newly born child sickened and died of fever and he himself came near to death. But nothing quenched his missionary zeal; and in 1846 he was rewarded by the arrival of a 'dear and long-expected fellow-labourer', Johann Rebmann, ten years his junior and his equal in enthusiasm.

Rebmann, like Krapf, came from Württemberg; but had been trained in a Church Missionary Society college in London. Almost at once the two men went down with fever, and when they had recovered they moved to Rabai, a higher and healthier spot. It was from Rabai that they made their amazing journeys. They went—as Livingstone went—in search of suitable sites for mission-stations; and even in the excitement of exploration they never forgot that, first and foremost, their job was to preach the Gospel.

Rebmann was the first to go. Armed only with a Bible and an umbrella and with eight unarmed porters he set out on

October 14th, 1847. He had no idea how far he would get but within five days he had covered about 100 miles and reached Mount Kadiaro, which no white man had seen before. Five days later he was back at Rabai, suffering from sore and swollen feet, but otherwise none the worse for his journey. The following year he embarked on a longer, far more dangerous enterprise. The Sultan's representative in the area, the governor of Mombasa, was alarmed to learn than an unarmed missionary proposed to travel through country haunted by fierce tribesmen and wild beasts. He warned Rebmann on no account to

ascend the mountain Kilimanjaro, because it is full of evil spirits. People who have ascended the mountain have been slain by the spirits, their feet and hands have been stiffened, their powder has hung fire, and all kinds of disasters have befallen them.

The warning was puzzling, and Rebmann was determined to find out exactly what it meant. With eight porters and a guide and with the inevitable Bible and umbrella he left Rabai on April 27th, 1848. It was the rainy season; and yet, despite heavy downpours of rain, he had passed Mount Kadiaro and within ten days was crossing the Jagga (Chagga) country round the lower slopes of Mount Kilimanjaro. 'How splendid the whole landscape,' he exclaimed, 'with its rich variety of mountain, hill, and dale, covered by the most luxurious vegetation! I could have fancied myself on the Jura mountains, near Basle, or in the region about Cannstatt in the dear fatherland.'

By now the guide was showing signs of nervousness. 'You are here with nothing but an umbrella,' he complained as they bivouacked under a tree, 'and formerly we needed five hundred muskets, so dangerous was the spot where we are; for this was one of the chief encampments of the plundering Kwavi.' Rebmann was fatalistic. 'It is the work of God,' he replied. 'He has opened a way for his Gospel.'

May 11th, 1848, was the date of Rebmann's great discovery.

This morning we discerned the mountains of Chagga more distinctly than ever; and about ten o'clock, I fancied I saw the summit of one of them covered with a dazzlingly white cloud. My guide called the white which I saw, merely 'Beredi', cold; it was perfectly clear to me, however, that it could be nothing else but snow.

And so this single-minded, devout missionary became the first white man to see the snowy dome of Kibo, highest summit of Mount Kilimanjaro. The discovery, to him, was but one among the many manifestations of God's goodness to man. 'Resting awhile soon afterwards under a tree, I read in the English Bible the CXIth Psalm, to which I came in the order of my reading.' The sixth verse, 'He hath shewed His people the power of His works, that He may give them the heritage of the heathen,' seemed particularly appropriate to the occasion as he meditated 'in sight of the magnificent snow-mountain.' Now, too, he understood the meaning of the governor's warning: those who had tried to climb the mountain had been killed, not by evil spirits but by the intense cold. What he could not know was that his discovery of a snow-mountain on the Equator would immediately spark off a bitter controversy. In England, a member of the Royal Geographical Society, Mr Desborough Cooley, sneered at Rebmann's report as 'a most delightful mental recognition only, not supported by the evidence of his senses'; and dismissed the claim that men had died from cold as 'a fireside tale'.

Rebmann remained in the district only long enough to nurse his torn feet and speak 'the chief articles of our faith' to the people; then, retracing his route to Mount Kadiaro, he returned to Rabai by a more southerly route.

In November of the same year he took the Chagga road again. He had heard that far beyond Kilimanjaro in the country of Unyamwezi (in what is now Tanzania) there was a vast inland sea. The discovery of this sea—Lake Tanganyika— would obviously be of great geographical importance; but, typically, the missionaries' journals refer to the paramount importance of opening up the country to Christian endeavour. Rebmann tried—but failed—to reach the lake, and struggled back to Rabai, a walking skeleton, wasted by fever, hunger and exhaustion.

He made no further journeys, but stayed at the mission-house, preaching, teaching, and translating the Bible. It was now Krapf's turn. In 1849, after a preliminary investigation of the foothills of the Usambara mountains to the south-west of Mombasa, as usual in search of sites for mission-stations, he turned north-west and followed Rebmann's route until he came in sight of Mount Kilimanjaro. He was informed by tribesmen that although many men had perished on the mountain a few had succeeded in collecting some of 'the silver-like stuff' which, 'when brought down in bottles, proved to be nothing but water'. Some of those who survived returned 'with frozen extremities' which the ignorant ascribed to the influence of evil spirits. 'All the arguments which Mr Cooley has adduced against the existence of such a snow-mountain,' wrote Krapf, 'and against the accuracy of Rebmann's report dwindle to nothing when one has the evidence of one's own eyes of the fact before one'.

Convinced that Rebmann's report was entirely truthful Krapf pushed north-westward into the country of the Wakamba people in what is now Kenya. He reached Kitui towards the end of November, and learned from the chief, Kivoi, who had himself been to the Chagga country and seen Kilimanjaro, of the existence of another snow-capped mountain 'six days journey from Kitui, which was called Kegnia'. Kivoi advised him to climb a hill above the village, and 'if the sky were clear I should be able to see the mountain'. It was the rainy season and the mountain was hidden; but on December 3rd, 1849, as Krapf was leaving Kitui, the rain-clouds suddenly lifted. 'I could see Kegnia most distinctly, and observed two large horns or pillars, as it were, rising over an enormous mountain to the north-west of the Kilimanjaro, covered with a white substance.'

So Krapf, too, joined the company of the great explorers.

Germany honoured him with a gold medal; France presented both men with silver medals: but in England, visited by Krapf in an attempt to interest the Church Missionary Society in his scheme for a chain of mission-stations across Africa, their discoveries were virtually ignored. Krapf was received by the Prince Consort; but he was given no official award, despite the fact that he had followed up the discovery of Mount Kenya by a survey of the whole coast from Mombasa to Cape Delgado on the borders of Mozambique. It was not until 1861 that the discovery of Mount Kilimanjaro was confirmed by the German explorer K.K. Von der Decken, who twice visited the area. On the second visit he climbed the mountain to a height of 14,000 feet but failed to reach the snow-line. Four years later he set out towards Mount Kenya, following the course of the River Juba; but was speared to death in the town of Bardera, in what is now the Somali Republic.

Krapf had been helped in his survey by a missionary colleague, J. J. Erhardt, who had joined the mission-station at Rabai in 1849. Erhardt also drew a map of the country between the coast and the vast inland sea in Unyamwezi which was to prove of the greatest value to future explorers. He went on several journeys into the interior: but Krapf, alone, made one more important discovery. In July, 1851, he left Rabai with permission to found a new station in Ukamba in the highlands to the north of Rebmann's original route to Kilimanjaro. At Kitui he was joined by Chief Kivoi and a number of his people. Their caravan was attacked by bandits armed with bows and poisoned arrows: Kivoi was killed and his party fled. On this occasion Krapf was carrying a gun as well as an umbrella, but he could not bring himself to do more than fire into the air. Then he ran for shelter. He realized that he could not be far from the River Tana; and he stumbled on the river almost by accident, 'not now impelled by geographical curiosity, but by extreme thirst.'

Broken in health, Krapf retired to his native Germany. There, he made a partial recovery, married for the second time, and settled down to his translations of the Scriptures into African languages. He returned several times to Africa and visited Rabai where Rebmann, now entirely alone and nearly blind, was still at work. This valiant man remained in Africa without a single break for nearly 30 years. He retired to Württemberg in 1875, to die a few months later near the home of his 'dear fellow-labourer' Krapf, who survived him by five years.

VIII

The Riddle of the Nile

LUDWIG KRAPF HAD a distant hope of solving the greatest of puzzles, the source of the Nile. This was not to be; but in 1853, soon after he left Rabai, he met in Cairo one of the men who made a contribution towards the solution and gave him a description of Kilimanjaro and Kenya and of the inland sea which Rebmann had failed to find.

The explorer was Richard Burton, one day to become famous for his translation of *The Arabian Nights*. Burton was a strange figure, romantic and sinister, with 'the brow of a god and the jaw of a devil', according to his friend the poet Swinburne. He was born in 1821, the son of an Army officer, and as a boy he was wild, undisciplined and pugnacious. He was educated partly in France, where his family was living, and later at Oxford University; and in the course of his career he was a soldier, explorer, archaeologist and author, as well as one of the greatest linguists and translators of his day.

As a young man serving in the Indian Army Burton learned Hindustani and a number of other Indian languages; but his chief love was Arabic, which he had begun to teach himself at Oxford. The Army made use of him in intelligence work; and he loved this cloak-and-dagger existence, for which he disguised himself as a merchant, wearing a false beard and hair and staining his naturally dark skin with henna. After a bad attack of cholera followed by a serious eye disease he was invalided out of the Army and retired to England with no prospect of employment, to write several books on India, its peoples and their customs, and to flirt with all the marriageable girls he met. While on a visit to France he noticed a handsome blonde girl of nineteen; and when he looked at her with his burning, magnetic eyes she fell madly and irrevocably in love. Her name was Isabel Arundell: and, as she correctly remarked to her sister, 'That man will marry me'.

Owing to the opposition of her mother they did not marry until 1861. Both before and after her marriage—a tempestuously happy one—Isabel had to endure many years of separation; for Burton would allow no one to interfere with his schemes. When they first met he was busily planning a secret expedition: by 1852 he had grown a beard, shaved his head, and vanished. His goal was Mecca, sacred city of Islam, which the Swiss explorer Burckhardt had entered 40 years before.

Since Mecca was forbidden to unbelievers, Burton spent a month in Alexandria, practising his Arabic and perfecting his disguise as a Muslim doctor: in this he was so successful that one of his patients offered him his daughter in marriage. He then travelled up the Nile to Cairo (where he met Krapf and revealed his true identity), unaware of the importance which the river was to assume in his life. After spending several weeks in Medina, which Burckhardt had also visited, he arrived undetected in Mecca and while carrying out the complicated ritual of prayer and observance demanded of a pious pilgrim, he contrived to examine the black stone in the famous shrine, said to have been given to the patriarch Abraham by the Angel Gabriel.

Burton spent nearly a week in Mecca; and on his return home he wrote a book, *The Pilgrimage to El-Medinah and Meccah*, a classic of its kind, which was extremely well received. Encouraged by the success of his disguise he was soon planning a second dangerous enterprise, a visit to the mountain city of Harar situated between Ethiopia and what is now the Somali Republic. Harar, home of fanatical Muslim Somali, was unknown to Europeans; and according to tradition the stronghold would lose its independence if ever an unbeliever entered it.

Disguised as an educated Arab merchant, Burton approached

the city, riding on a white mule with gaudy trappings. He was escorted into the presence of the Emir, who reclined on a divan, the handle of a scimitar protruding from the cushions. The audience chamber was festooned with weapons, chains and instruments of torture; and the Emir was flanked by a guard of half-naked warriors. He stared suspiciously at the visitor and reminded him of the legend of the city's threatened independence. Burton knew that recognition would mean death; but after a prolonged and sickening silence the Emir graciously extended his hand and a smile softened his face. 'This smile, I must own, was a relief,' was Burton's laconic comment. He had, he continued, been 'prepared for the worst, and the aspect of affairs in the palace was by no means reassuring'.

Days of anxiety and tension followed. The Emir was clearly suspicious and Burton was shadowed by spies. He was, however, able to make an unobtrusive study of the city and its people; but when he finally emerged unscathed from the stronghold he was greeted by his native guard as one risen from the dead.

Burton now rejoined his own party, the members of which included an Englishman, John Hanning Speke, surveyor, geologist and botanist, and six years younger than Burton. Speke, blue-eyed with a tawny beard and hair, was as different from Burton in character as in appearance. His ancestors had lived for generations in Somerset in the West Country, and as a boy he had lived an open-air life, preferring birds-nesting and hunting to school. Like Burton, he had served in the Indian Army, and had spent his leaves hunting big game in the Himalayas. He was on his way to East Africa to collect specimens of rare animals and birds when he met Burton in Aden; and he abandoned his own plans to join forces with the older man.

Burton was the leader of the party which was exploring Somaliland. In the early days of their association Speke admired him tremendously. Yet, even on this first expedition there was friction, the result of the contrast between Burton's arrogant, swashbuckling behaviour and Speke's extreme reticence. This friction was brought to a head by a most unpleasant incident. In April, 1855, they were camping on a ridge above the Red Sea port of Berbera when they were attacked during the night by a band of Somali. The native guard fled in panic: one of the English members of the party was killed: and Speke, who was hit by several well-aimed stones, instinctively moved backwards towards his tent. 'Don't step back,' cried Burton, 'or they'll think we are retiring.' Goaded, Speke turned to the attack; but he was felled by repeated blows from a war-club and stabbed as he lay on the ground in the arms and legs. Burton, a javelin thrust through his jaw from cheek to cheek, fought his way out and escaped to the coast. The javelin was removed by some British sailors; but Burton, whose jaw had been badly injured, remained scarred for life and looked more sinister than ever. Despite his wounds Speke, with the one surviving Englishman, struggled to the coast. He was too badly wounded for further exploration and so the party had to return home. Speke was mentally as well as physically hurt. He never forgot that Burton had indirectly accused him of cowardice; and although he said nothing at the time the accusation continued to fester in his mind.

In spite of his bitterness against Burton Speke was ready to join forces with him again. At the end of 1856, after both men had served in the Crimean War, they returned to Africa. They were backed by the British Foreign Office and the Royal Geographical Society. Their instructions were to find the true source of the Nile, making first for the Sea of Ujiji, an enormous lake of unknown size, which, it was hoped, would prove to be their goal; and then, if possible, to go north in search of another reported lake. While he was in Harar, Burton had asked a number of questions about the Nile; and in Cairo Krapf had spoken about the river and the mysterious Mountains of the Moon. He was aware of the claims which had been made by Fathers Paez and Lobo and by James Bruce. From the evidence he was convinced of the accuracy of the Jesuits' reports; and,

James Grant

John Hanning Speke

while he thought Bruce guilty of exaggeration, he believed that fundamentally he had told the truth. Nearly 90 years had passed since Bruce's adventures in Ethiopia; and geographers had at last begun to suspect that he might have been right. Of course, as we saw, he had seen the source of the Blue Nile, not that of the parent stream, the White Nile. The whole course of the White Nile had never yet been explored, and geographers did not know if it had one source or two.

When Burton and Speke landed at Zanzibar they met the missionary Johann Rebmann, who warned them that the route they intended to take from Mombasa to the interior was infested by tribes of warlike Masai. They decided, instead, to start from Bagamayo, a more southerly point on the coast.

They were delayed for six months in Bagamayo, engaging porters and buying supplies, and recovering from a bad bout of fever. Burton spent his convalescence learning the Kiswahili tongue, spoken in the interior; but Speke, who could not speak Arabic or any other foreign language, was unable to communicate with any of the people they encountered except by signs. This made him suspicious not only of Arabs and Africans but also of Burton, whom he suspected of conspiring against him. In the course of their 1,000-mile journey into the interior the two men grew to hate one another. Speke, who had once admired and respected Burton, now found him impossibly arrogant and dictatorial: Burton found the younger man sullen and secretive.

Even if they had remained the best of friends the journey would have been difficult in the extreme. The porters made repeated efforts to run away; the pack-animals died from tsetse fly disease; and the explorers themselves were tormented by other biting insects. Their valuable scientific instruments and most of their provisions were lost; and since they now had no spare clothes and the ones they were wearing were torn to pieces by thorns, they were reduced to wearing makeshift garments sewn from blankets. The route to what is now Tabora in central Tanzania took them from the coastal cliff area through a vast region of steaming jungle, with bogs waist-deep in mud and thick with hidden tree roots; and over three mountain ranges. First one man, then the other, went down with fever; and Burton was so weak he could scarcely walk. It took them 134 days to cover the 600 miles to Tabora. There, Arab traders confirmed a rumour they had already heard that there was not one immense slug-shaped lake, as shown on Erhardt's map, but several lakes, two of them extremely large. The lakes might be linked by a river; but no one knew whether they were or not.

Burton decided that the most westerly lake was probably their goal. Long before they reached it he was so wasted by fever that he could not walk but had to be carried in a litter. Both he and Speke had developed an eye disease, and Speke had temporarily become half blind. They struggled on another 400 miles until, on February 10th, 1858, Burton recorded, 'walls of sky-blue cliff with gilded summits' came in view. They climbed a steep, stony hill; and, gazing downwards through a curtain of trees, he saw something glinting. 'What is that streak of light which lies below?' he asked their Arab guide. 'I am of opinion that that is *the* water,' the man replied. It was in fact the Sea of Ujiji (Lake Tanganyika). From the hilltop it looked small and insignificant, for they could see only a small corner; and Burton was half inclined 'to propose an immediate return, with a view to exploring the Nyanza, or Northern Lake. Advancing, however, a few yards, the whole scene suddenly burst upon my view, filling me with admiration and delight.'

Burton and Speke were the first Europeans to discover the world's longest freshwater lake, 'a blue gem set in a deep crater of yellow sandstone rock.' The wonder was hidden from Speke. 'From the summit of the Eastern horn,' he wrote, 'the lovely Tanganyika Lake could be seen in all its glory by everybody but myself.'

They clambered down the hillside and came to the settlement of Ujiji on the eastern shores of the lake. It was a large village of beehive shaped huts with a slave market and an abundance of fresh food for sale—milk, chickens, eggs and vegetables. Burton and Speke were anxious to explore the lake, especially when they heard that some Arab slavers had been to the northern end and had seen a large river—the Rusizi—flowing out of it. This, thought the explorers, might prove to be the Nile. They were warned, however, that they might not return alive: the tribes living on the opposite shore were cannibals; and those at the northern end of the lake were cannibals of an even more ferocious kind.

Despite this warning Burton and Speke hired two canoes and some boatmen, who paddled them across the lake and along the western shore. The lakeside tribes, wrote Burton, were clearly examining them 'in the light of butcher's meat'; but did not attack them. They landed at a village not far from the northern end of the lake. There they met the Arab traders who had seen the Rusizi, and who now insisted that the river entered the lake and did not flow out of it. Burton would have gone on to check this statement; but the boatmen, terrified of being eaten, insisted on going back. And so they returned to Ujiji with the problem of the Nile source unresolved.

Burton, who was still very sick, suggested giving up and returning to the coast; but Speke, who had recovered his sight, was bent on obeying instructions and discovering the northern lake which, according to the rumour, was larger even than Tanganyika. Burton therefore agreed to wait while Speke went on alone. They retraced their footsteps to Tabora: and, after sixteen days of amazingly easy travel, Speke arrived at the shores of a lake so vast that he was assured that it 'probably extended to the end of the world'. He had, in fact, found the greatest of all the African lakes, an inland sea of 26,000 square miles. From the rumours and clues he had gathered he was convinced that this lake, which he named Victoria, was the 'fountain-head of that mighty stream that floated Father Moses on his first adventurous sail—the Nile'. He was certain that he had 'solved a problem which it had been . . . the ambition of the first monarchs of the world to unravel'. He was right, but he had no proof: and when, after examining only a minute section of the southern end of the lake, he returned triumphantly to tell Burton that he had discovered the source of the Nile, Burton was exceedingly sceptical. He would not agree to Speke's suggestion that they should make a thorough investigation of the lake. They must go home, he insisted, adding, according to Speke's account, that when they had completely recovered their health and got some more money they could 'return together, and finish our whole journey'.

Relations between the two men were now more strained than ever. On the journey back to the coast Speke was sick and delirius: and Burton, who nursed him, had to listen to his feverish wanderings. In his delirium Speke raved against Burton, accusing him—not without cause—of being unbearably proud and patronizing; he railed against him for refusing to believe that Lake Victoria was the true source of the Nile; and relived the incident of Burton's tacit accusation of cowardice.

They took four months to reach the coast, completing a journey which had lasted just under two years. Speke, who was by now much better in health, decided to go straight home; but Burton, worn out in mind and body, decided to spend a few days in Aden. Outwardly the two men appeared to be on good terms; and, according to Burton, Speke undertook to await his arrival in London so that they could make a joint report to the Royal Geographical Society.

In the event, when Burton reached London 12 days later he found that Speke had already reported his discovery and his theory to Sir Roderick Murchison, the President; and, at Sir Roderick's request, he had lectured to members of the Society. He had made such an excellent impression that funds were already being collected to send him back to Africa, with the object of returning to Lake Victoria and, if he found an outlet at its northern end which could be the Nile, of following the course of the river wherever it might lead. The route of this proposed expedition would lie through unexplored country; and it was hoped that Speke would not only settle the problem of the Nile source but also discover the exact whereabouts of the Mountains of the Moon. Speke and Burton disagreed about the precise locality of these mountains: Speke believed them to be a fairly low range near the northern end of Lake Tanganyika; Burton placed them further north and east—between Lake Victoria and the Upper Nile.

Speke's second-in-command was his friend, Captain James Grant, a former officer in the same regiment of the Indian Army. Grant, a gentle, modest man of Speke's own age, was never likely to question his leadership nor to claim any honour or glory for himself.

Burton, who was not even invited to join the expedition, suggested that there should be two, the parties starting from different points. His idea was turned down. It is true that he was awarded the Founder's Medal of the Royal Geographical Society; but it was clear that the Society was far more interested in Speke's discovery of Lake Victoria than in the discovery of Lake Tanganyika. Burton was hurt and angry. He would have been more angry still had he known that both in private and in public Speke was spitefully pulling his achievements and his character to pieces. In the fall of 1859 Speke published a series of articles in which he emphasized the importance of his own discovery and played down the importance of Burton's. He miscalculated the exact position of Lake Victoria on the map; claimed that a river which he had heard about but had not seen was probably the Nile; and insisted that the elusive Mountains of the Moon were in fact the ranges near Lake Tanganyika. Burton, on the other hand, remained firm in his conviction that the Mountains of the Moon were snow-capped mountains further to the north and east.*

The position of the Mountains of the Moon was only one of the points at issue between Burton and Speke. Burton, who now believed that there were probably four great lakes in

---

* In 1889 the Mountains of the Moon were proved by the explorer Henry Morton Stanley to lie north and west. They were the snow-capped Ruwenzori range, their tallest peaks rising to a height of some 17,000 feet. Cf. page 150.

Central Africa, longed to prove that Lake Tanganyika was the source of the Nile. In his book *Lake Regions in Central Africa*, published in 1860, he did not stake a firm claim but he did not actually deny it. And in his natural resentment against Speke he accused him of being 'unfit for any other but a subordinate capacity', and criticized the haste with which he had appeared before the Royal Geographical Society, 'thus taking measures to secure for himself the right of working the field I had opened. . . .'

Speke and Grant left for Africa before Burton's book appeared; Livingstone was already in Africa, in the region of Lake Nyasa; Burton alone was left behind, sullen and furious. He had spent a great deal of his own money on his African adventure and was now in need of paid employment. The only post he was offered was an inferior one, as British Consul on the Spanish-owned island of Fernando Po, the island from which the Lander brothers had sailed for England 30 years earlier.

Burton, who loathed Fernando Po, went exploring in the Niger delta. He also climbed Mount Victoria, a hitherto un-scaled mountain in the Cameroon range of Southern Nigeria, commenting that 'to be first in such matters is everything, to be second nothing'. He continued his explorations throughout his period as Consul, recording a great deal of valuable information about the country, the people and their customs.

Speke and Grant meanwhile were deep in their travels. They took the old route to Tabora and then struck northward into the unknown native kingdoms of Uganda. Rumanika, the King of the kingdom of Karagwe, gave them a great welcome. He was a man with many wives, all famous for their size. The women, fed entirely on milk, were so colossally fat that they could not stand upright but flopped around on the ground like animals.

Grant, who had a poisoned leg, remained in Karagwe while Speke went on to the kingdom of Buganda on the northern shore of Lake Victoria. Mutesa, the King of Buganda, was a tall, good-looking young man, who wore his hair cropped short except on the top of his head where it was combed into a high ridge. He was elegantly dressed, wrapped in a cloak of finely stitched antelope skins, with rows of beads round his throat and ankles and a ring on every finger and toe. Mutesa, courteous in manner, was a tyrant in action. 'Majesty in Uganda is never satisfied,' wrote Speke in his *Journal of the discovery of the source of the Nile*, 'till subjects have grovelled before it like the most abject worms.' He was horrified to see how cheaply life was held. He had presented the King with a rifle, which Mutesa had loaded and handed to a page with orders to go and shoot a man in the outer court. Presently the page returned and proudly announced his success. 'And did you do it well?' asked the King. 'Yes, capitally,' the page replied. No one thought—or dared—to enquire who the dead man might have been.

The death of one man was nothing to Mutesa. His subjects were tortured and killed at his slightest whim not in ones but in hundreds. Under the influence of wizards, sorcerers and medicine-men, fearful atrocities were committed; and on state occasions as many as 2,000 victims were sometimes sacrificed. Yet, with all its barbarity, Buganda had a civilization of its own. The King was an absolute despot; but below him there existed a chain of representatives each with certain responsibilities and powers. No man could appeal against the King's edicts; but Mutesa, though capable of the vilest acts, possessed a sense of justice, and for the most part he was simply repeating savage practices initiated by his predecessors.

Speke spent three months at Mutesa's court before he was joined by Grant, still limping but otherwise in good health. On the journey from Karagwe both men had crossed a river, the Kagera. Since this river flowed into Lake Victoria, not out of it, they knew that it could not be the Nile: but at Mutesa's court they learned of the existence of a great river to the east of the Kagera which flowed out of the lake. This, they decided, must be the Nile and they were eager to trace it. Mutesa was most reluctant to let them go; but by July 17th, 1862, they had gained his consent and departed in a caravan with an escort.

Two days later they separated. Speke sent Grant westward towards the kingdom of Bunyoro, while he himself turned eastward towards the river, determined to reach it alone.

If Grant was disappointed that Speke had deprived him of the chance of reaching the longed-for goal he never showed it: he was utterly loyal to his friend. When, later, he was asked for an explanation of Speke's extraordinary behaviour he let it be assumed that he was still too lame to have kept up with his leader.

Speke, with his escort, reached the Nile on July 21st, at Urondogani, some forty miles downstream from Lake Victoria. 'Here at last,' he wrote, 'I stood on the brink of the Nile; most beautiful was the scene, nothing could surpass it! It was the very perfection of the kind of effect aimed at in a highly developed park; with a magnificent stream, 600 to 700 yards wide, dotted with islets and rocks. . . .'

He followed the river upstream and on July 28th, after 'crossing hills and threading huge grasses, as well as extensive village plantations lately devastated by elephants . . . we arrived at the extreme end of the journey. . . . We were well rewarded.' He had arrived at the waterfall by which the river emerged from the northern shore of the lake.

> Though beautiful, the scene was not exactly what I had expected; for the broad surface of the lake was shut out from view by a spur of hill, and the falls, about 12 feet deep, and 400 to 500 feet broad, were broken by rocks. Still it was a sight that attracted one to it for hours—the roar of the waters, the thousands of passenger-fish, leaping at the falls with all their might, the Wasoga and Waganda fishermen coming out in boats and taking post on all the rocks with rod and hook, hippopotami and crocodiles lying sleepily on the water, the ferry at work above the falls, and cattle driven down to drink at the margin of the lake,—made, in all, with the pretty nature of the country—small hills, grassy-topped, with trees in the folds, and gardens on the lower slopes—as

interesting a picture as one could wish to see. The expedition had now performed its functions. I saw that old father Nile without any doubt rises in the Victoria N'anza [Lake], and as I had foretold, that lake is the great source of the holy river which cradled the first expounder of our religious belief.

Speke named the falls the Ripon Falls, after Lord de Grey and Ripon, President of the Royal Geographical Society when 'my expedition was got up'.

A month later Speke joined Grant in Bunyoro, whose King, Kamrasi, kept them for some weeks in semi-captivity. There they learned of the existence of a lake to the north-west of Lake Victoria; and it seemed possible that this lake might prove to be a second source of the Nile. Speke made no attempt to find it: instead he went northward towards Gondokoro, an Arab slaving station on the White Nile, in the Sudan, where it had been arranged for fresh porters and supplies to await him. By this time he had lost most of his possessions: both he and Grant were tired men, and an additional journey into the unknown might well have endangered their lives.

It took them three months to reach Gondokoro. When they rejoined the river and tried to float down stream they were soon forced back on land by cataracts and had to toil onwards on foot. They reached Gondokoro on February 13th, 1863, nearly two and a half years from the start of their journey.

To Speke's intense annoyance the porters and supplies had not arrived. Instead, he had an unexpected meeting with another British explorer. This was a burly big-game hunter and traveller, Samuel White Baker, who had a passion for exploration.

Baker, a man of 42, had lived for some years in Ceylon where his hunting trips had taken him deep into unknown country. After a spell in England, during which his wife had died, he had set out on his wanderings; and in Hungary he met and married Florence von Sass, a slim, boyish-looking but beautiful girl fifteen years his junior. The Bakers were in Ethiopia exploring the Nile tributaries when they learned that two white men had been detained on the Upper Nile. These men, thought Baker, must be Speke and Grant, now long over-due and feared to be dead. He therefore decided to go to Gondokoro and meet them on their northward journey and started up the river with three ships and 100 men. He had considerable trouble with the ships, and also with the men who proved to be unreliable and threatened to mutiny. Baker was a masterful man, very ready to use his fists; and peace was restored only through the intervention of his wife, a woman of great courage and charm, the ideal wife for a hot-tempered man. Baker had the greatest admiration for her serenity and powers of endurance. 'Possessing a share of sang-froid admirably adapted for African travel,' he wrote in his book *Albert N'yanza: Great Basin of the Nile*, 'Mrs Baker was not a *screamer*, and never even whispered; in the moment of suspected danger, a touch of my sleeve was considered a sufficient warning.'

When they reached Gondokoro on February 15th, 1863, Baker wrote,

> my men rushed madly to my boat with the report that two white men were with them who had come from the *sea*! Could they be Speke and Grant? Off I ran, and soon met them in reality; hurrah for old England! They had come from the Victoria N'yanza from which the Nile springs. . . . The mystery of ages was solved.

Baker found Speke

> excessively lean but in reality . . . in good tough condition; he had walked the whole way from Zanzibar. . . . Grant was in honourable rags; his bare knees projecting through the remnants of trousers that were an exhibition of rough industry in tailor's work. He was looking tired and feverish,

but both men had a fire in the eye, that showed the spirit
that had led them through.

Speke was deeply moved by the encounter. He himself
wrote:

> What joy was this, I can hardly tell. We could not talk fast
> enough, so overwhelmed were we both to meet again. Of
> course we were his guests in a moment and learnt everything
> that could be told. I now first heard of the death of H.R.H.
> the Prince Consort . . . then there was the terrible war in
> America. Baker then said he had come up . . . expressly to
> look after us, hoping, as he jokingly said, to find us on the
> equator in some terrible fix that he might have the pleasure
> of helping us out of it.

Baker, in fact, was longing to undertake an independent
piece of exploration. 'Does not one leaf of the laurel remain for
me?' he asked. Speke then told him of the undiscovered lake
and his theory that it might prove to be a second Nile source.
He gave him a map of the area on which the supposed position
of the lake was marked; and then, saying goodbye to the
Bakers, Speke and Grant departed on the last stage of their
northward journey, leaving Baker to take up the search for the
new lake.

The Bakers, who left Gondokoro in March, 1863, in a small
caravan, were obliged to join forces with a notorious band of
slave traders, since no one else was familiar with the country
through which they had to pass. 'The traders,' complained
Baker, 'convert every country into a wasp's nest—they have
neither plan of action nor determination.' He himself, 'being
unfortunately dependent upon their movements, am more like a
donkey than an explorer, that is saddled and ridden away at a
moment's notice.'

By the following February, however, they had arrived at the
capital of King Kamrasi of Bunyoro, who refused to allow them

to go on to the lake. They argued; and Kamrasi, taking advantage of his powerful position, proceeded to extort from Baker pretty well everything he possessed, finishing with a demand for Florence. Baker was outraged.

> If this were to be the end of the expedition, I resolved it should also be the end of Kamrasi, and drawing my revolver quietly, I held it within two feet of his chest, and looking at him with undisguised contempt, I told him that if I touched the trigger, not all his men could save him: and that if he dared to repeat the insult I would shoot him on the spot. . . . My wife, naturally indignant, had risen from her seat, and, maddened with the excitement of the moment, she made him a little speech in Arabic (not a word of which he understood), with a countenance almost as amiable as the head of Medusa.

Mrs Baker's tirade was supplemented by one from her maid, who

> had appropriated the insult to her mistress, and . . . also fearlessly let fly at Kamrasi, translating as nearly as she could the complimentary address that 'Medusa' had just delivered. Whether this little *coup de théâtre* had so impressed Kamrasi with British female independence that he wished to be let off his bargain, I cannot say, but with an air of complete astonishment, he said 'Don't be angry! I had no intention of offending you by asking for your wife; I will give you a wife, if you want one, and I thought you might have no objection to give me yours; it is my custom to give visitors pretty wives, and I thought you might exchange. Don't make a fuss about it; if you don't like it, there's an end of it; I will never mention it again!' This very practical apology I received very sternly, and merely insisted on starting.

They did start then, with an escort of three hundred of Kumrasi's men, who deserted day by day until only twelve remained. The small party now had to cross a river at a point where 'thickly-matted water-grass and other aquatic plants' formed 'a natural floating bridge'. Baker led the way, telling his wife to follow in his track. When he had gone about a quarter of the way he looked back and was horrified to see her sinking slowly into the weeds, her face distorted and purple. As he looked she fell as though shot. In a minute he was at her side, and with the help of his men 'dragged her like a corpse through the yielding vegetation, just keeping her head above the water: to have carried her would have been impossible, as we should all have sunk together through the weeds'.

Florence had sunstroke; and when they reached the other side she was placed on a litter and 'carried mournfully forward as a corpse'. Sick himself and torn with anxiety, Baker walked beside the litter,

> through the long day's march over wild park-lands and streams, with thick forest and deep marshy bottoms; over undulating hills, and through valleys of tall papyrus rushes, which, as we brushed through them . . . waved over the litter like the black plumes of a hearse.

Night after night he watched over her as she tossed in delirium. But Florence Baker, for all her slight appearance, had a tough constitution. During the very night her husband believed she was dying she began to recover, although she remained sick and weak for the rest of the journey. 'God alone knows what helped us,' wrote Baker thankfully. 'The gratitude of that moment I will not attempt to describe.'

Now at length they were nearing the lake. For years, he wrote,

> I had striven to reach the 'sources of the Nile'. In my nightly dreams during the arduous voyage I had always failed, but after so much hard work and perseverance the cup was at my very lips, and I was to *drink* at the mysterious fountain before another sun could set—at the great reservoir of Nature that ever since creation had baffled all discovery.

And then, on March 14th, 1864,

having crossed a deep valley between the hills, we toiled up the opposite slope. I hurried to the summit. The glory of the prize burst suddenly upon me! There, like a sea of quicksilver, lay far beneath the grand expanse of water—a boundless sea horizon on the south and south-west glittering in the noon-day sun; and on the west, at fifty or sixty miles' distance, blue mountains rose from the bosom of the lake to a height of about 7,000 feet above its level.

It is impossible to describe the triumph of that moment;— here was the reward for all our labour . . . England had won the sources of the Nile!

Long ago, he added, he had 'arranged to give three cheers with all our men in English style in honour of the discovery'; but he was too overcome with emotion 'to vent my feelings in vain cheers for victory'. Instead, he helped his wife down the hill to the lakeside and drank his own toast in lake water. As a memorial to Queen Victoria's husband he named his find Lake Albert. 'The Victoria and the Albert lakes,' he wrote, 'are the two sources of the Nile.'

Baker was wrong in thinking that Lake Albert extended a vast distance to the south. In reality he was very near the southern end, and what he took to be lake water was the River Semliki which links Lake Albert with a lake which had yet to be discovered, Lake Albert Edward. He had added a vital link to Speke's discovery; but, to be strictly accurate, Lake Albert is not, as he wished to believe, the second source of the Nile. The lake is watered from Lake Albert Edward by the Semliki, and from Lake Victoria by the Victoria Nile (marked on Speke's map as the Somerset); and the entire White Nile, which flows out of the northern end of Lake Albert, originates in Lake Victoria. Neither Speke nor Baker was to map out the whole Nile system: this task was left to Henry Morton Stanley.

The Bakers, exhausted, sick and short of supplies as they now were, paddled and sailed along the eastern shore in roughly-made boats for 13 days until they reached Magungo at the head of the lake, the entrance of the Victoria Nile. Travelling a short distance up the crocodile-infested river they came to a huge waterfall. 'This,' wrote Baker, 'was the greatest waterfall of the Nile, and, in honour of the distinguished President of the Royal Geographical Society, I named it the Murchison Falls, as the most important object throughout the entire course of the river.' And then, after further dangers and adventures, he and his intrepid wife arrived back at Gondokoro: they had been absent for two and a half years.

At Cairo, on the homeward journey, Baker learned that he had been awarded the Gold Medal of the Royal Geographical Society for his

> vigorous exploration, entirely at his own cost, in the interior of Africa . . . for having fitted out an expedition by which he relieved Speke and Grant; and . . . for his noble endeavour to complete the discoveries of those travellers. . . .

He also received a knighthood and other honours; and his books, *The Albert N'yanza, Great Basin of the Nile*; and *Nile Tributaries of Abyssinia*, published in 1866 and 1867 respectively, read like the most exciting kind of adventure stories and were exceedingly popular.

In 1863, when the Bakers set off to find Lake Albert, Speke and Grant returned to England and a chorus of praise. The trouble between Speke and Burton was now coming to a head. Speke had not traced the course of the Nile northward from Lake Victoria, and Burton was prepared to do his utmost to demolish Speke's theory that the Nile had its source in Lake Victoria and also his description of the importance and size of the lake.

In August, 1864, a little over a year since Speke and Grant's return, Burton arrived in London. Burton and Speke each had his own adherents, and the idea was put forward that the two men should argue their respective theories in public. There was some suggestion that Livingstone, who was in London at the time, should take the chair at the meeting, but this came to nothing. Livingstone was convinced that Speke was wrong, for he believed that the Nile rose, not in Lake Victoria, but far away to the south. 'Poor Speke,' he wrote, 'has turned his back upon the real sources of the Nile. . . . His river at Ripon Falls was not large enough for the Nile.'

A debate between Burton and Speke was arranged for the next meeting of the British Association for the Advancement of Science to be held in the city of Bath. Burton was far from sure that he wanted to take part. Then he was told that Speke was going about saying, 'If Burton appears on the platform at Bath I will kick him.' 'Well,' replied Burton, 'that settles it. By God, he shall kick me!'

In an effort to demolish Speke's theory and to substantiate his own, Burton prepared a sketch map which showed Lake Tanganyika, with its feeder streams, as the true source of the Nile, and Lake Victoria simply marked as the 'supposed site' of a lake. In Burton's map the River Rusizi was shown flowing northward out of Lake Tanganyika and entering Lake Albert. It will be remembered that when Burton and Speke had tried to get to the northern end of Lake Tanganyika they did not see the river for themselves, but they were assured that it flowed into and not out of the lake, which meant that it could not be the Nile. Burton was now ready to believe that this information was false. His map showed an outlet from Lake Albert flowing on to Gondokoro, and this, he declared, would prove to be the real Nile.

Burton went down to Bath with his wife, who had been trying to bring about a reconciliation between the two men. On the day before the debate there was a preliminary meeting of the British Association. Burton and Speke, coming face to face, cut one another dead, but Burton noticed that his rival looked nervous and ill. The meeting began, and Burton saw some one beckon to Speke from the back of the hall. Speke

Emin Pasha

Samuel Baker

Florence Baker

stood up, and exclaiming 'I can't stand this any longer' abruptly left the hall. Next day, when Burton arrived for the great debate, he learned that Speke was dead. He had gone out shooting that morning and was climbing a wall when his shot-gun went off, killing him instantly.

The verdict given at the inquest was 'accidental death'; but many people thought that Speke had killed himself rather than face his rival. The truth will probably never be known. The devoted Grant, who had not uttered a word against him, Sir Roderick Murchison and David Livingstone attended his funeral. Speke was only 37 when he died: the tragedy was that he had been right all along although he could not prove it. His great discoveries are commemorated on a granite obelisk which stands in London's Kensington Gardens, with an inscription reading: 'In memory of Speke, Victoria, Nyanza and the Nile'.

The controversy about the Nile sources continued after Speke's death, Burton clinging obstinately to his own theory until it was finally demolished by Stanley. Burton never returned to Central Africa. He continued to travel, to write, and to translate, his frank translation of the *Arabian Nights* making him rich, as well as famous. In 1886 he received a knighthood, a belated tribute to his achievements, and he died in 1890. He certainly ranks among the greatest of Africa's explorers; and as a scholar and writer he is outstanding.

IX

'How I Found Livingstone'

IN 1869, FIVE years after Speke's death, Baker returned to Africa, this time in the service of the Egyptian Government, as Governor-General of the Equatorial Nile basin. He was the first Englishman to hold high office under the Egyptian Government: his task was to bring the country south of Gondokoro under Egyptian authority; to suppress the slave trade and replace it by regular commerce. He found that this involved him in fighting, not only with the slave traders but also with Kamrasi's son Kabarego, who had succeeded his father as king of Bunyoro. By the end of his four-year term of office Baker had succeeded in driving the slavers from the region of the Nile south of Gondokoro, and had established the framework of an administration for his famous successor General Gordon. He lived on till 1893, and when he died, an old man of 82, his beloved Florence was at his side.

Baker was remembered in Africa as a powerful man, over forceful but scrupulously just. He had a number of critics, among them the German explorer and botanist Dr Georg Schweinfurth, who was convinced that in driving away the slavers Baker had done more harm than good. The slavers, Schweinfurth argued correctly, might be driven out of one place but they simply carried on their operations elsewhere.

Between 1869 and 1870 Schweinfurth examined the western affluents of the Upper Nile, whose importance he thought had not been fully appreciated by Baker and Speke. The chief value of Schweinfurth's work lies really in his book, *The Heart of Africa* (published in England in 1873) which gives a clear and vivid description of the country through which he travelled.

Schweinfurth's work was later amplified by another German, Dr Wilhelm Junker, who extended the scope of his investigation of the Nile affluents.

In the meantime, in an obituary oration on Speke delivered at the Royal Geographical Society, Sir Roderick Murchison had announced that he proposed to send Livingstone back to try to solve the outstanding problems concerning the waterways of Central Africa. This delighted Livingstone, who was longing for a chance to discover the Nile source for himself, and believed that the northward flowing River Lualaba would prove to be the Nile.

The plan of Livingstone's last expedition, which started in 1865, was to explore the watersheds of the Nile, the Congo and the Zambezi. 'I hope,' wrote Livingstone, 'to ascend the Rovuma or some other river north of Cape Delgado, and, in addition to my other work, shall strive, by passing along the northern end of Lake Nyasa and round the southern end of Lake Tanganyika, to ascertain the watershed of that part of Africa.'

It was an ambitious plan and Livingstone was in no fit state to carry it out. When he started he had with him, among others, two Africans, Susi and Amoda, who had been with him on the Zambezi, and two boys whom he had rescued from slave raiders in the Shire Highlands, one of whom—Chuma—was to remain with him to the end. Throughout, Livingstone was dogged by bad luck. The porters proved unwilling and unreliable: the Arab traders became increasingly hostile; and Livingstone, revolted by the cruelty of the slavers and by scenes of carnage which he could not prevent, grew more and more depressed, while his failing health was made more precarious by the loss of his medicine chest. Yet he persisted. As planned, he made his way up the Rovuma River, but when the time came to cross Lake Nyasa he could find no one to help him and was obliged to march round the southern tip of the lake and then march north-west in the direction of Lake Tanganyika. On this journey he reached an undiscovered lake—Lake Mweru

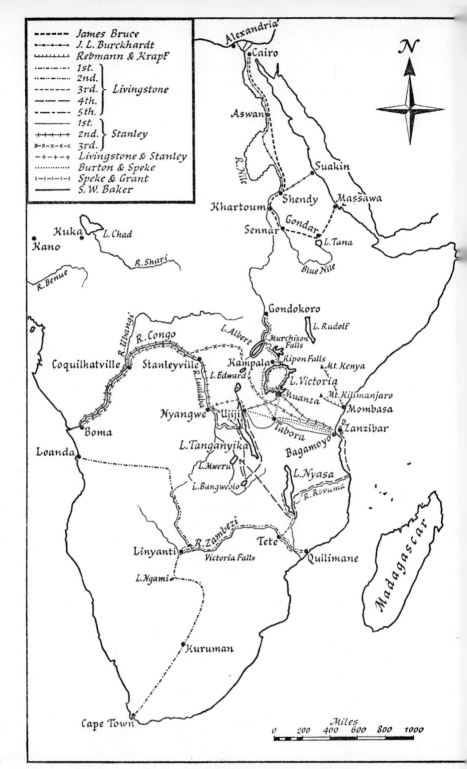

- - - - -	James Bruce
+—+—+	J. L. Burckhardt
+++++++	Rebmann & Krapf
-·-·-·-	1st.
-··-··-	2nd.
- - - -	3rd. } Livingstone
—— ——	4th.
— — —	5th.
————	1st.
+++++++	2nd. } Stanley
x—x—x—x	3rd.
-+-+-+-	Livingstone & Stanley
··········	Burton & Speke
⌐-⌐-⌐-⌐	Speke & Grant
————	S. W. Baker

N

Alexandria
Cairo
Aswan
Suakin
Massawa
Shendy
Khartoum
Gondar
Sennar
L. Tana
Blue Nile
R. Nile

Kuka
L. Chad
Kano
R. Shari
R. Benue

Gondokoro
L. Rudolf
L. Albert
Murchison Falls
R. Congo
Ripon Falls
R. Ubangi
Kampala
Mt. Kenya
Coquilhatville
Stanleyville
L. Edward
L. Victoria
R. Lualaba
Muanza
Mt. Kilimanjaro
Nyangwe
Ujiji
Mombasa
Tabora
Zanzibar
Boma
L. Tanganyika
Bagamoyo
Loanda
L. Mweru
L. Nyasa
L. Bangweolo
R. Rovuma

Linyanti
R. Zambezi
Tete
Victoria Falls
Quilimane
L. Ngami

Madagascar

Kuruman

Cape Town

Miles
0 200 400 600 800 1000

EXPLORERS IN SOUTHERN AFRICA

—near the effluence of the River Lualaba; and also discovered Lake Bangweolo, some 80 miles to the south of Mweru and linked to it by river. Then he struggled on to the western shore of Lake Tanganyika and crossed the lake to the town of Ujiji. There he rested, too weak to march another step. By this time rumours of his death, spread by porters who had deserted the expedition, had begun to reach England. Eager for a journalistic scoop, the *New York Herald* decided to send its star reporter Henry Morton Stanley to Central Africa to find out if the rumours were true.

Stanley, in some ways the greatest of Africa's explorers and certainly the most spectacular, had triumphed over a childhood as horrifying as any described in the novels of Charles Dickens; and his defects were the direct result of his determination to live it down. He was born in 1841 in the town of Denbigh in Wales, the illegitimate son of a cottager, John Rowlands, whose name he was given. His father died not long after he was born, and his mother went to London to find work as a domestic servant, leaving him in the care of relations who deposited him at the age of five in the parish workhouse. The workhouse had a school of sorts; and for nine years young John Rowlands was bullied and beaten by a sadistic, half-lunatic school-master, who ended his days in a home for the insane. Even at the height of his fame Stanley was to be tormented by memories of the past, and by one incident in particular. One of his friends, a boy whom he described as 'king of the school for beauty and amiability', died very suddenly. John Rowlands, with one or two of the other boys, crept into the mortuary where the body lay, turned back the sheet which covered it and found to their horror that it was disfigured with welts and bruises.

Rowlands endured these gruesome conditions until he was fifteen and then he rebelled. Threatened with yet another flogging, he rounded on the savage master, beat him unconscious, and escaped from the workhouse by climbing over the wall. Reluctantly, his relations took him in, but they made it clear that they did not want him. He left Denbigh for Liverpool, where he lodged with a married aunt and found work in a shop.

The wages were very poor; he was not paying his way, and so at eighteen he joined an American ship as cabin boy. Life on board was tough, nearly as tough as it had been in the workhouse, and at New Orleans, cheated out of his wages, he deserted. Work was now imperative, and he boldly accosted a kindly looking stranger and asked for a job. This man, a cotton-broker, not only found work for the boy but took him into his home and gave him his own names—Henry Morton Stanley. Young Stanley spent two years working and travelling with his new father in preparation for a business career. Then the older Stanley died, leaving the son he had not formally adopted rudderless and alone.

On the outbreak of the Civil War Stanley enlisted in the Confederate Army. He was captured at the battle of Shiloh and, in exchange for a promise of release, agreed to join the Federal Army. But he fell sick almost at once and as soon as he had recovered he was discharged from further service. In the autumn of 1862 he sailed for England, turned up unexpectedly at his mother's home, and was promptly thrown out. Feeling more bitter than ever towards his family and the country which had disowned him, he worked his passage back to America. After several sea voyages he joined the Federal Navy as a ship's writer; and during the expeditions against Fort Fisher he sent despatches to the newspapers which the editors accepted and printed.

On his discharge from the Navy at the end of the war Stanley decided to become a full-time journalist. He quickly made good; and joined the staff of the *New York Herald* in 1868. The Livingstone assignment, one of several important assignments entrusted to Stanley, was arranged in Paris by James Gordon Bennett, the manager, son of the owner. Stanley later described the interview with Bennett in his famous book, *How I Found Livingstone*. To Bennett's question, 'Where do you think Livingstone is?' he replied:

'I really do not know, Sir.'

'Do you think he is alive?'

'He may be or he may not be,' I answered.

'Well, I think he is alive, and that he can be found, and I am going to send you to find him. . . . Draw a thousand pounds now,' he said, 'and when you have gone through that, draw another thousand, and when that is spent, draw another thousand, and when you have finished that, draw another thousand, and so on; but FIND LIVINGSTONE.'

Stanley, then, was to have unlimited funds; but before going to look for Livingstone he was instructed to attend the inauguration of the Suez Canal; go up the Nile and find out all he could about Samuel Baker's expedition into Upper Egypt; visit Jerusalem, Istanbul, the Crimea, the Caspian Sea, and Iran; and thence to India.

'When you have come to India, you can go after Livingstone. Probably you will hear by that time that Livingstone is on his way to Zanzibar; but, if not, go into the interior and find him if alive. Get what news of his discoveries you can; and, if you find he is dead, bring all possible proofs of his being dead. That is all. Good night, and God be with you.'

'Good night, sir,' I said: 'What it is in the power of nature to do I will do; and on such an errand as I go upon, God will be with me.'

Stanley faithfully fulfilled his various assignments, sending back despatches to the *Herald*. It was not until January 6th, 1871, more than 14 months since his meeting with Bennett, that he arrived in Zanzibar to begin his search. He stayed with the American Consul, for he considered himself entirely American; and he was so keen to get a scoop that he refused to divulge his plans to John Kirk, now British Consul. His caravan was large and well equipped, and although he marched right through the rainy season his pace was very much faster than Livingstone's or Burton and Speke's. At 30, he was in splendid physical form. He was a harsh disciplinarian who drove his men desperately hard. Every morning he roused the caravan with a crack 'like a pistol-shot' of 'the Great Master's donkey-whip'. He had no time for slackers. 'When mud and wet sapped the physical energy of the lazily-inclined,' he noted, 'a dog-whip became their backs, restoring them to a sound, sometimes to an extravagant activity.' The two European members of the party, both from Stanley's point of view thoroughly unsatisfactory, died on the journey, unable to stand the furious pace.

Stanley's journal, which he was to write up in book form on his return, was dramatic and sensational.

No living man, or living men shall stop me, only death can prevent me. But death—not even this; I shall not die, I cannot die! And something tells me, I do not know what it is . . . something tells me tonight I shall find him, and— write it larger—FIND HIM! FIND HIM! Even the words are inspiring. I feel more happy. Have I uttered a prayer? I shall sleep calmly tonight.

Death did not prevent him. From information he received he learned that Livingstone was alive and at Ujiji: and there, in the presence of a crowd of interested spectators, the famous meeting took place. 'As I advanced slowly towards him,' wrote Stanley,

I noticed he was pale, looked weary, had a grey beard, wore a bluish cap with a faded gold band around it, had on a red-sleeved waistcoat and a pair of grey tweed trousers. I would have run to him, only I was a coward in the presence of such a mob—would have embraced him, only, he being an Englishman, I did not know how he would receive me. So I did what cowardice and false pride suggested was the best thing—walked deliberately up to him, took off my hat and said: 'Dr Livingstone, I presume?' 'Yes,' said he with a kind smile, lifting his cap slightly. I replace my cap on my head, and he puts on his cap, we both grasp hands and I say aloud—'I thank God, Doctor, I have been permitted to see you.' He answered—'I feel thankful that I am here to welcome you.'

Stanley spent four months with Livingstone, whose health and spirits rapidly revived. They were memorable months for Stanley, who learned to love and revere the older man and to find in him the ideal father figure. Livingstone grew fond of Stanley, although in character he was entirely different. Livingstone was paternal, loving and endlessly patient with his African followers. Stanley, who had boundless confidence in the superiority of the white man over the coloured, was insensitive, hard and dictatorial. It amused him, for instance, to recall a conversation he overheard between Livingstone's servants and his own. ' "Your master," say my servants to Livingstone's, "is a good man, a very good man; he does not beat you, for he has a kind heart; but ours—oh! he is sharp—hot as fire". '

During his months with Livingstone, Stanley questioned him about his discoveries and theories and asked if he had explored the northern end of the lake, from which Burton claimed the Rusizi emerged. Livingstone replied that he had not, since he was convinced that the Lualaba, away to the south-west, would prove to be the Nile and that Lake Tanganyika could not therefore be the source of the river. 'Well, if I were you, Doctor,' Stanley advised, 'before leaving Ujiji, I should explore it, and resolve the doubts upon the subject.'

Livingstone agreed; and the two men went by canoe to the upper end of the lake. Livingstone discovered at once that Burton was wrong: the Rusizi flowed southward into the lake— as Burton and Speke had been told—and so could have no connection with the drainage system of a major river flowing northward.

More than ever convinced that he was right, Livingstone was eager to return to the Lualaba to complete his work. He refused to accompany Stanley back to England; but accepted his offer of porters and supplies from his own store. He gave Stanley his papers, which included a letter to the *New York Herald*. In this he gave a harrowing description of the massacre by slavers of hundreds of people at Nyangwe on the Lualaba and of other atrocities committed in the area of Ujiji. 'If my disclosures regarding the terribly Ujijan slavery should lead to the suppression of the East Coast slave trade,' he wrote, 'I shall regard that as a greater matter by far than the discovery of all the Nile sources together.'

He was still determined to find the Nile sources, however, and turned southward once more. 'Oh, how I long to be permitted by the Overpower to finish my work,' he wrote. It was not to be. In April, 1873, he was halted by mortal sickness near the village of Ilala, not far from Lake Bangweolo. There the faithful Susi and Chuma found him early one morning, as they had left him the previous night, kneeling by his camp-bed. His face was still buried in his hands as though in prayer; but he was dead.

Then began a final journey as heroic as any of Livingstone's own. Susi and Chuma, with some sixty other stalwarts, buried the great man's heart under a tree, embalmed his body, and wrapped it to resemble a bale of cloth, for they were well aware that they would encounter tribes who believed that a dead body was a symbol of misfortune. Then, carrying their burden lashed securely to a pole, they set out on the 1,500 mile march to the east coast. The journey took them over 10 months: but they would not relinquish the body until they reached Bagamoyo and could hand it over to British officials from Zanzibar.

The body was taken to England; and on April 18th, 1874, it was carried to its final resting-place in London's Westminster Abbey. Among the pall-bearers, all of whom had played a part in Livingstone's story, were Stanley, Kirk, and Jacob Wainwright, one of the men who had carried the body on its miraculous journey to the coast.

The lettering on Livingstone's grave commemorates this journey as well as his own:

Brought by faithful hands over land and sea here rests David
Livingstone, missionary, traveller, philanthropist, born
March 19, 1813, at Blantyre, Lanarkshire, died May 1,
1873, at Chitambo's village, Ulala.

A bronze statue of Livingstone, dressed as Stanley described
him, stands outside the Royal Geographical Society's hall in
London. It honours a man who spent thirty years of his life
exploring Africa and endeavouring to convert the African tribes
to Christianity. If he failed to discover the sources of the Nile,
it was his campaign against slavery, reinforced by Sir John Kirk,
which drove the Sultan of Zanzibar to forbid the export of
slaves throughout his East African dominions and to close the
slave market for ever.

X

The Main Story Completed

EXPLORATION OF THE lake areas of Central Africa was not yet complete. Before the news of Livingstone's death had been confirmed, two relief expeditions were sent out from England to find him. The first, starting from the west coast, got no further than Salvador. The second, led by a naval officer, Lovett Cameron, started from the east coast. Cameron met Susi and Chuma at Tabora in October, 1873. They convinced him that they were carrying Livingstone's body; but he decided to push on to Ujiji to collect Livingstone's papers. This done, he explored and mapped the greater part of Lake Tanganyika and discovered the Lukuga River; and, from his observations on the Lualaba, he came to the conclusion that it was not the Nile but part of the Congo system.

Ten years had now passed since Speke's death but his discoveries had yet to be confirmed. Exploration proceeded and fresh clues were found under the authority of General Gordon who, by this time, had succeeded Baker as Governor General of Egypt's province, the Equatorial Nile basin. In 1874 Colonel Chaillié-Long, an American attached to Gordon's staff, established that Lakes Victoria and Albert are linked by the Somerset (or Victoria) Nile; and he examined Kioga, a shallow lake on the Nile which lies between Lake Victoria and Lake Albert.

Among those who tackled the remaining problems was the picturesque Emin Pasha, linguist, scientist and doctor, medical officer on Gordon's staff. Emin Pasha was really Eduard Schnitzer, a German Jew who had become a Muslim; and Gordon was so impressed by his administrative gifts that he appointed him governor of Sudanese Equatoria. Between 1877 and 1888 Emin Pasha travelled widely in the regions around Lake Albert and discovered the River Semliki which enters the lake at its southern end. Yet, despite all the work which had been done, the overall problems still remained. Was Lake Victoria one lake or several linked lakes? And was it indeed the true source of the Nile? These problems were left to Stanley.

Although the meeting with Livingstone was the high spot in Stanley's life it was only the beginning of his career as an explorer. His famous greeting—'Dr Livingstone, I presume'— echoed round the world; and, while some people found it wholly admirable, others rocked with laughter at its utter incongruity. Stanley, who had no sense of humour, would have disowned the remark if he had not already given it credence in *How I Found Livingstone*; and it continued to embarrass him to the end of his days.

When he arrived in England in May, 1872, he was given a tremendous reception and awarded the coveted Gold Medal of the Royal Geographical Society. His book was an instantaneous success; and the press as a whole praised his magnificent achievement. And yet in several newspapers there were hints that his journey—if it had ever taken place at all—was no more than a journalistic stunt and that Livingstone's letter to the *New York Herald* was a forgery. Stanley, never a popular figure, added to his unpopularity by publicly attacking Sir John Kirk who had, he maintained 'let Livingstone down' by failing to send him fresh porters and supplies.

But Stanley was determined to confound his critics by showing them that he was capable of still greater achievements. In 1874 he persuaded the editors of the *New York Herald* and London's *Daily Telegraph* to finance another trip to Africa. His instructions were 'to complete the work left unfinished by the lamented death of Dr Livingstone; to solve, if possible, the remaining problems of the geography of Central Africa; and to investigate and report upon the haunts of the slave traders' at Ujiji on Lake Tanganyika and Nyangwe on the Lualaba. Stanley interpreted this directive as permission to make a thorough investigation of Lakes Victoria and Tanganyika and of the whole of the western area of Central Africa between the Lualaba and the Atlantic Ocean. Speke, it will be remembered, had discovered the Ripon Falls by which he claimed the Nile emerged from Lake Victoria: Burton still clung to his theory that the Rusizi was the Nile and that it flowed out of Lake Tanganyika: Livingstone had died persisting that the Lualaba was really the Nile. Stanley, like Lovett Cameron, suspected that the Lualaba was part of the Congo, and he realized that in order to establish their identity he might have to cross the continent.

The caravan which left Zanzibar in November, 1874, was larger and better equipped than any that had gone before. Stanley had recruited 356 Africans, some of whom had been with him on the Livingstone expedition, and three young Englishmen, who had no special qualifications. They were Frederick Barker, a clerk in a London hotel, and two brothers, Edward and Francis Pocock, the sons of a Kentish fisherman. The expedition was equipped with a wooden boat, the *Lady Alice*, which could be taken to pieces and reassembled; eight tons of stores and five dogs.

Still only 33, Stanley was in first-class condition and ready to set a gruelling pace. He was prepared for heavy losses; and indeed before he reached Lake Victoria some 14 weeks later he had lost no fewer than 181 of his men. Some had died from disease; some had been killed in fights with hostile tribes; some had deserted. He had also lost Edward Pocock, who had died of typhus.

The expedition reached Lake Victoria on the south-eastern shore, near the spot from which Speke had first seen the lake and surmised that it must be the source of the Nile. Surmises were not enough for Stanley. He gave orders for the *Lady Alice* to be put together and on March 8th, 1875, leaving the two Englishmen in charge of the main party, he set sail with ten carefully picked Africans. 'The men were rather downhearted and rowed reluctantly,' he noted, 'as we have had many a grievous prophecy that we shall all drown in the Lake, or die at the hands of some ferocious people living on the shores of the Nyanza.'

Alternately sailing and rowing up the eastern shore of the lake they reached Speke's Ripon Falls on March 28th. They were now coming into the area ruled by King Mutesa of Buganda; and on April 4th Stanley was received in audience by Mutesa in his capital, built on the site of the modern city of Kampala. The King was now in his early forties, and Stanley, whose impression was very different from Speke's, succumbed to his well known charm. He found the tyrant 'a most intelligent, humane and distinguished prince . . . not a tyrannous savage, a wholesale murderer, but a pious Mussulman, and an intelligent humane King reigning absolutely over a vast section of Africa, loved more than hated, respected more than feared, of all his subjects'.

Stanley was hopeful that Mutesa would give up the Muslim faith and become a Christian, and Mutesa declared himself perfectly willing to listen to Bible readings. In fact, however, he had changed little since Speke had met him: he had merely become more diplomatic and, since he realized that he had much to gain from friendship with the great Powers, he was careful to conceal any evidence of his customary brutalities.

Anxious to complete the circumnavigation of Lake Victoria, Stanley took to the water again, and by May 5th he was back at his starting point after a voyage of 1,000 miles. He had proved conclusively that Lake Victoria was not a chain of lakes but one vast inland sea. He had also proved that it had a single major outlet, at the Ripon Falls; and one major intake, the Kagera, which Speke and Grant had dismissed as a possible source of the Nile. 'Speke,' wrote Stanley, 'has now the full glory of having discovered the largest inland sea on the continent of Africa, also its principal affluent as well as its outlet.' If he was sure in his own mind that Speke's river was indeed the Nile, he had not yet finally disposed of Burton's claim on behalf of the Rusizi.

On his return trip from Buganda Stanley had been attacked by hostile tribes. During his absence there had been a number of casualties in the camp. The young clerk Frederick Barker had died of fever: so, too, had a number of Africans, while others were sick or had deserted. Mutesa, however, had promised him reinforcements, and when these arrived he embarked on a series of reprisal raids against the offending tribes which would have horrified the humane Livingstone. In one of these raids—on a tribe at the head of the lake—he actually joined forces with the tyrant Mutesa. The King would have liked him to remain in Buganda; but Stanley refused to be detained. Instead, he explored the country to the west of Lake Victoria and discovered a smaller lake just below the Equator, Lake Edward. Then, after visiting the ageing King Rumanika, he travelled southward to Ujiji. In June, 1876, the *Lady Alice* was launched on Lake Tanganyika. By the end of July Stanley was back at his starting point, with positive proof that there was no outlet which could conceivably be identified with the Nile.

So now, having disposed once and for all of Burton's claim, Stanley turned his attention to Livingstone's theory and followed the valley of the River Luama from Lake Tanganyika to its confluence with the Lualaba. It was now October 1876, and he was about to embark on his greatest venture: if Livingstone had been right his theory must be proved; if wrong, the connection between the Lualaba and the waterways of Central Africa must be determined. 'The great mystery that for all these centuries Nature had kept hidden away from the world of science was waiting to be solved,' wrote Stanley in his book *Through the Dark Continent*. 'Now before me lay the superb river! My task was to follow it to the Ocean.'

The vast district around Nyangwe, where Livingstone had witnessed the terrible massacre, was controlled by an enterprising and enormously wealthy Arab slave trader Mohammed bin Sayed (or Tippu Tib as he was called). Tippu Tib was willing to furnish Stanley with porters in return for a large sum of money; and Stanley started his journey with 356 men, some of whom brought their wives along.

The first stage of the journey took them overland, for the lower reaches of the river were blocked by impassable cataracts. For fourteen days they struggled through a forest so thick and dark that Stanley often found it impossible to write in the journal from which his book was to be compiled. They passed through several native villages, and it was plain, from the skulls and bones scattered around the cooking-sites, that the inhabitants were cannibals. When at length they emerged from the forest and camped for the first time on the right bank of the river, Stanley at once decided to rename the Lualaba the Livingstone. 'Downward it flows to the unknown,' he wrote in his usual dramatic vein. 'Tonight black clouds of mystery and fable, mayhap past the lands of the anthropoids, the pigmies and the blanket-eared men . . . I seek a road. Why, here lies a broad water cleaving the Unknown to some sea, like a path of light. . . .'

The *Lady Alice* was now launched on the river highway, with some thirty men aboard, the remainder walking along the river bank. Stanley did not know where the river would take them, but he was full of confidence. Throughout the voyage, perhaps the most heroic in the whole history of African travel, the expedition met disasters of every kind. Almost at once the men began to fall sick with smallpox, dysentery and typhoid fever, and there were several deaths every day. On land, the legs and feet of the marchers were torn by thorns and deep, painful ulcers developed which made walking impossible. Stanley therefore commandeered several canoes which had apparently been abandoned on the river and lashed them together to form a floating hospital.

Before long they came again to an impassable stretch of water. It proved to be one of many. Each time the boats had to be taken to pieces and hauled overland along a path which the men had to hack through the bush. And repeatedly, on land and on the water, they were attacked by cannibal tribesmen.

Stanley's party had firearms to protect them; but the cannibals, who did not understand their danger, attacked again and again, driven not only by the desire for human meat but also by the very natural suspicion that no one but a slaver would brave such a journey.

At first the river carried them in a northerly direction and it seemed possible that Livingstone had been right after all. By now they were coming to the first of seven cataracts, to be known to posterity as the Stanley Falls. As they hewed a path round one cataract after another a rear-guard kept off the attacks of the marauding tribesmen. Each time they emerged from the forest to a stretch of calm water the men hoped that their troubles were over; but each time their hopes were dashed by the thunder of yet another waterfall. Weary and disheartened, the men were growing mutinous. Stanley kept them moving by his own example of strength and endurance and, when all else failed, by threats.

By the end of January, 1877, they had passed the seventh cataract and come to an unobstructed stretch of river on the Equator, at a point where one day the town of Stanleyville would be built. They were no longer travelling north but northwest, and Stanley was almost certain that they were not on the Nile but on the Congo. If this were so, he knew that they had months of travel before them: he knew, too, since the river was still high above sea-level, that further waterfalls lay ahead. But there could be no turning back. Livingstone, he wrote,

called floating down the Lualaba a foolhardy feat. So it has proved, indeed, and I pen these lines with half a feeling that they will never be read by any man; still, as we persist in floating down according to our destiny, I persist in writing, leaving events to an all-gracious Providence. Day and night we are stunned with the dreadful drumming which announces our arrival and presence on these waters. Either bank is equally powerful. To go from the right bank to the left is like jumping from the frying-pan into the fire. As we row down amongst these islands, between the savage countries on either side of us, it may well be said that we are 'running the gauntlet'.

By early February they had also run out of food; and Stanley decided that even at the risk of being killed and eaten they must try and barter with one of the tribes. They still had some suitable gifts—cloth, wire and beads; and the offer of these, coupled with overtures of peace, gained them some provisions. Stanley asked the chief the name of the great river. He replied that it was called the Kongo: there was no longer any doubt of its identity.

By February 18th they had travelled in a wide arc and were again on the Equator, a little below the modern town of Coquilhatville. They were now heading south-west: and once again, since they had run out of food, they took the risk of approaching one of the tribes. By good luck they had found a friendly village; and from that time onwards they were not attacked. After resting in the village for a few days they went on and soon came to a lake in the river which Frank Pocock, who had shown great powers of endurance, suggested should be called Stanley Pool.

The distance between the pool and the Atlantic coast was only a few hundred miles; but Stanley had been right in judging that there must be dangerous rapids ahead. At one point the *Lady Alice*, with Stanley on board, nearly capsized; and when the men saw that their leader was safe, they

rushed up one after another with their exuberant welcome to life which gushed out of them in gesture, feature, and voice. And Frank, my amiable and trusty Frank, was neither last nor least in his professions of love and sympathy, and gratitude to Him who had saved us from a watery grave.

The rapids continued, and by April 21st they had covered a distance of only 34 miles. They knew now that they could not be very far from the sea, for the native people had samples of European goods. But this hopeful sign meant that there was no longer any demand for their own goods, and once more they were nearly starving. Some 30 of the men deserted, and deaths from disease and hunger were growing more numerous. To Stanley's deep distress, Frank Pocock, who had endured all his sufferings without complaint and was crippled by ulcers on his legs and feet, was drowned in a treacherous stretch of water. In his honour Stanley named the spot Pocock Basin.

By the beginning of August Stanley had come to the conclusion that they must abandon the boats and strike overland to the coast where he knew he would find Portuguese traders. He was himself so weak and exhausted that he asked a friendly chief to go on ahead with a letter addressed 'to any gentleman who speaks English'. In it he explained that he had travelled from Zanzibar and had with him '115 souls', including 13 women and the children born to them on the way; and, he continued:

> We are now in a state of imminent starvation. We can buy nothing from the natives, for they laugh at our kinds of cloth, beads, and wire. There are no provisions in the country that may be purchased, except on market days, and starving people cannot afford to wait for these markets.

He asked for rice or grain for his men and, for himself, a little tea, coffee, sugar and biscuits. And he signed the letter 'H.M. Stanley, Commanding Anglo-American Expedition for Exploration of Africa', adding that if any one doubted his identity he was the man who had found Livingstone in 1871.

Within two days a letter reached him to the effect that supplies were on the way. On August 9th, 1877, 'on the 999th day of our departure from Zanzibar', the remnants of the expedition staggered into the little settlement of Boma. More than half the original party had perished, and Stanley, although only 36, was white-haired and haggard. When, however, he turned for a final look at the river,

I felt my heart suffused with purest gratitude to Him whose hand had protected us, and who had enabled us to pierce the Dark Continent from east to west, and to trace its mightiest River to its Ocean bourne.

On the 1000th day of the voyage the surviving members of the party were put on board a ship which would take them back to Zanzibar by way of the Cape. Stanley alone took ship for England, his task completed.

There was no longer any doubt that the Nile rose in Lake Victoria to flow northward on its way to the Mediterranean; nor that the Lualaba joined the Congo to flow across Africa to the Atlantic.

Certain gaps in geographical knowledge remained and Stanley himself helped to fill them. He was most anxious to persuade the British Government to open up the Congo basin by road and railway from the west coast to Stanley Pool where the river became navigable. He was unable to do this, and so he offered his services to King Leopold II of the Belgians, who was not so hesitant. On behalf of the King and of the International African Association which he had founded, Stanley returned to the Congo in 1878 to undertake the organization of the vast region into what became known as the Congo Free State (now the Congo). While he was there—in 1883—he discovered two more lakes, Timba and Leopold II.

His work was supplemented among others by the remarkable Italian-born explorer Savorgnan de Brazza. In 1875 de Brazza explored the greater part of the Ogowe in the Gabon in French Equatorial Africa (now Gabon); and discovered the Rivers Alima and Likona, tributaries of the Congo.

Stanley returned to Africa for the last time in 1887. His task was to relieve Emin Pasha, who had been left isolated by the murder of General Gordon in 1885 and by the withdrawal of the Christian missionaries who had gone to Buganda but had been expelled by Mutesa's successor. Stanley approached the area from the west coast, travelling through the great forests of the Congo. Having rescued Emin Pasha—who showed no desire to be rescued—he went on to discover the snow-capped Ruwenzori Mountains—the legendary Mountains of the Moon —midway between Lake Albert and Lake Edward, which he had discovered on his earlier journey. And then, with Emin Pasha, he made his way to the east coast and Zanzibar.

He had thus crossed Africa from east to west and from west to east; and this last journey was a fine ending to his career as an explorer. After his return to England he was knighted and settled down to a brief career as a Member of Parliament and to marriage. He and his wife had no children and so they adopted a son, whose upbringing could scarcely have been more different from his own. He died in 1904 at the age of sixty-four.

All the important information about the sources of the Nile had now been revealed: it remained only to add certain details. Among those who played a part was a young Scotsman, Joseph Thomson. In 1879, at the age of 21, Thomson explored Central Africa between Lakes Nyasa and Tanganyika and discovered Lake Rukwa. In 1882 he returned to Africa in order to find a trade route from the east coast to Uganda. He pushed inland to Mounts Kilimanjaro and Kenya and then passed safely through the country of the warlike Masai to the north-eastern end of Lake Victoria.

Thomson was an explorer in the old tradition, driven by sheer curiosity and a love of travel. 'I am doomed to be a wanderer,' he wrote shortly before his death in 1895, 'I am not an empire-builder. I am not a missionary. I am not truly a scientist. I merely want to return to Africa and continue my wanderings.'

To us today the explorers seem like a race apart. They were men of the highest courage, with the strongest possible sense of purpose. They were willing to risk their health and their lives, to endure privation and years of separation from their families, to look for no rewards. They had one ambition in common: the honour and glory of helping to fill the blank spaces on the map of Africa. This ambition apart, their personal motives differed.

To Bruce, for example, the driving force was scientific curiosity and the need to escape from an intolerable burden of unhappiness: to Laing and Caillié it was the lure of the fabulous city of Timbuktu: to Burton, the desire to understand and identify himself with civilizations other than his own: to Stanley it was a determination to triumph over his wretched childhood and prove to himself and the world that he was among the great: to the missionaries Krapf and Rebmann it was a desire to spread the Gospel: and to Livingstone, perhaps the most heroic of them all, it was a love of the African peoples, a determination to strike a blow at the slave trade and to 'make an open path for Christianity and Commerce'. To all of them, to quote Richard Lander, 'there was a charm in the very sound of Africa', whether they had a definite object in view or, like Thomson, simply wanted to wander.

Exploration continued into the twentieth century but by the end of the nineteenth century the era of wandering was over. Once the main geographical problems had been solved and it had been proved that a market existed for African products it was almost inevitable that the great Powers should intervene and thrust their way in to exploit the country the explorers had opened. The international 'Scramble' which started in 1884 was precipitated by Stanley's second journey; for it was this journey, resulting as it did in the creation of the Congo Free State which led directly to the partition of Africa.

TABLE OF DATES

1613   Pedro Paez discovers the source of the Blue Nile.
1770   James Bruce at the source of the Blue Nile.
1796   Mungo Park reaches the Niger.
1823   Oudney and Clapperton discover Lake Chad.
1826   Laing visits Timbuktu.
1830   Richard and John Lander trace the course of the
        Niger.
1848   Rebmann discovers Mount Kilimanjaro.
1849   Krapf discovers Mount Kenya.
1851   Barth discovers the Upper Benue.
1851   Livingstone discovers the Zambezi.
1855   Livingstone discovers the Victoria Falls.
1858   Burton and Speke discover Lake Tanganyika.
1858   Speke discovers Lake Victoria.
1862   Speke discovers the Ripon Falls.
1864   Baker discovers Lake Albert.
1871   Stanley finds Livingstone.
1874–77 Stanley solves the outstanding problems of the Nile.

SUGGESTIONS FOR FURTHER READING

Brodie, Fawn M. *The Devil Drives: the Life of Sir Richard Burton*. New York: Norton, 1967

Bovill, E. W. *The Niger Explored*. Oxford: Oxford University Press, 1968

Crone, G. R. *The Explorers: Great Adventurers Tell Their Own Stories*. New York: Crowell, 1963

Divine, Arthur D. *Six Great Explorers*. New York: Dufour, 1954

Gardner, Brian. *The Quest for Timbuctoo*. New York: Harcourt, Brace and World, 1968

Moorehead, Alan. *The Blue Nile*. New York: Harper, 1962

Moorehead, Alan. *The White Nile*. New York: Harper, 1960

Oliver, Roland, and C. *Africa in the Days of Exploration*. New York: Prentice-Hall, 1965

Perham, Margery and Simmons, Jack, eds. *African Discovery*. Evanston, Illinois: Northwestern University Press, 1963

INDEX

Abyssinia—*see* Ethiopia
Africa, Arabs and, 13–14, 16, 73, 98, 113, 121, 144; British and, 18, 21, 41, 62, 95; Carthaginians and, 10–11; Dutch and, 18, 21, 94–6, 102; Egyptians and, 9–11, 16; French and, 18, 92–3; Greeks and, 10; Phoenicians and, 10; Portuguese and, 16–19, 21, 94, 98–100, 148; Romans and, 11–13; peoples of, 28, 30, 33, 47–8, 61–3, 65–6, 68–9, 71, 73, 75–6, 78–9, 84–5, 94–5, 97–100, 102–4, 106, 113, 120, 142–50; 'Scramble' for, 93, 151
African Association, 42–3, 49–50, 55, 58, 82
Albert, Lake, 126–8, 140–1, 150
Albert Edward, Lake, 126
Alima river, 149
Aswan, 11, 20, 24, 38, 55
Atbara river, 38

Badagri, 68, 71, 76
Bagamayo, 113, 138
Baikie, W. B., in North and West Africa, 91
Balugani, L., 23, 25, 29, 33, 39
Banks, Sir J., 41–3, 49–52, 55, 58
Baker, Florence, in Central Africa, 122–7, 130
Baker, Sir S. W., 135, 140; in Central Africa, 121–7, 130;

and *Albert N'yanza : Great Basin of the Nile*, 122, 127; and *Nile Tributaries of Abyssinia*, 127
Bangweolo, Lake, 133, 138
Bantus, the, 94–5, 97–8
Barker, F., 142, 144
Barrow, Sir J., 58, 68, 70
Barth, H., in Asia Minor, 83; in North Africa, 83–9; and *Travels and Discoveries in North and Central Africa*, 85–6, 89–91
Beurmann, M. von, in North Africa, 89
Bello, Sultan of Sokoto, 62–3, 67–71, 87
Benin, Bight of, 67–8, 82
Benue river, 71 *n*, 78, 86, 90–2
Biafra, Bight of, 68
Binger, L-G., 83; in North and West Africa, 92–3
Bornu, 58, 60, 69, 84–6, 88, 92–3
Brazza, P. S., de, 149
British Association for the Advancement of Science, 128–9
Bruce, J., 22, 38–9, 41, 56, 94, 102, 112–13, 151; in Egypt, 23–4; in Ethiopia, 25–34; in the Sudan, 34–7; and *Travels to Discover the Source of the Nile*, 27, 39, 102
Burckhardt, J. L., 110; in the Middle East, 55–6; and the Niger problem, 56
Burton, Isabel, 109–10, 128

Burton, Sir R., 109, 127–9, 135, 137, 142–4, 151; in the Middle East, 109; in Ethiopia and the Somali Republic, 110–11; in East Africa, 112–16; in West Africa, 118; and *The Arabian Nights*, 109, 129; and *The Pilgrimage to El-Medinah and Mecca*, 110; and *Lake Regions in Central Africa*, 118

Bushmen, 94

Bussa, 53, 68, 69, 77

Caillié, R., 64, 87–8, 91, 151; in North Africa, 72–5; and *Travels through Central Africa to Timbuktu*, 74–5

Cairo, 20, 24, 37–8, 42, 55, 92, 109–10, 112, 127

Cam, D., on West African coast, 17

Cameron, L., in Central Africa, 140, 142

Campbell, —, in North Africa, 56

Cape Town, 21, 94–6, 98

Chad, Lake, 58–60, 63, 68, 76, 85–6, 89, 92–3

Chaillié-Long, C., in Central Africa, 140

Chobe river, 98

Chuma, 131, 138, 140

Church Missionary Society, 102–3, 107

Clapperton, H., 59, 63–5, 82, 84, 87; in North and West Africa, 59–63, 67–71; and *Records of Captain Clapperton's Last Journey*, 75–6

Congo, 149–151

Congo river, 17–18, 42, 56, 131, 140, 142, 146–9

Decken, K. K. von der, in East Africa, 107

Denham, D., 70; in North Africa, 59–60; and *Narrative of Travels and Discoveries in Northern Nigeria*, 63

Dias, B., voyage round the Cape, 17

Dochard, —, in North and West Africa, 56, 73

Edward, Lake, 144, 150

Emin Pasha—*see* Schnitzer, E.

Erhardt, J. J., 114; in East Africa, 107

Esther, Princess, 27, 34

Ethiopia, 10–11, 18–20, 24, 25–34, 39, 92, 102, 110, 113, 122

Fernando Po, 81, 118

Fez, 14, 75, 91

Fezzan, the, 43, 57, 61, 70

Fulani, the, 61–2, 73

Gabon, 149

Galla tribes, 28, 30, 33, 102

Gama, V. da, voyage to India, 17

Gambia river, 18, 42–4, 49–52, 56, 73

George III, 23–5, 38

George IV, 67

Ghana, 93

Ghat, 60, 84–5

Gish, 29–30

Gondar, 20, 26, 29–30, 33

Gondokoro, 121–3, 127–8, 130

Gordon, General, in Central Africa, 130, 140, 149

Grant, J., in East Africa, 117, 123, 129, 143

Gray, W., in North and West Africa, 56, 73
Guinea, Gulf of, 9, 17–18, 53, 55, 68

Harar, 110–112
Hausa, the, 61, 63, 68, 71, 78–9
Henry, Prince of Portugal, 16–17
Herodotus, 10–11
Hornemann, F., in North Africa, 43
Hottentots, the, 94
Houghton, —, in North and West Africa, 43–5, 49

Ibn Battuta, 14
Ivory Coast, 93

Johnson, Dr, 39
Juba river, 107
Junker, W., in North Africa, 131

Kabara, 66–7, 74–5
Kabarego, king of Bunyoro, 130
Kadiaro, Mount, 104–5
Kagera river, 119, 143
Kalahari Desert, 96–7
Kamba, the, 103
Kamrasi, king of Bunyoro, 120–121, 123–4, 130
Kano, 61–3, 65, 69, 71, 84–5, 88
Kenya, Mount, 106–7, 109, 150
Khartoum, 10, 19, 37
Kikona river, 149
Kilimanjaro, Mount, 104–7, 109, 150
Kioga, Lake, 140
Kirk, Sir J., 100–1, 135, 138–9, 141
Krapf, J. L., 109–10, 112, 151; in Ethiopia, 102; in East Africa, 103–7

Krump, T., in Ethiopia, 20, 35
Kuka, 63, 85–6, 92
Kwavi, the, 104

Laing, A. G., 69, 75, 82, 87, 92, 151; in North and West Africa, 58–9, 63–7
Lander, J., 118; in North and West Africa, 76–82; and *Journal of an Expedition to explore the Course and Termination of the Niger*, 82
Lander, R. L., 83, 118; in North and West Africa, 68–72, 76–82; and *Journal of an Expedition to explore the Course and Termination of the Niger*, 82, 151; and *Records of Captain Clapperton's Last Expedition*, 75–76
Ledyard, J., in North Africa, 42
Leo Africanus, and *History and Description of Africa*, 14, 57, 63
Leopold II, King of the Belgians, 149
Leopold II, Lake, 149
Libyan Desert, 42–3, 92
Limpopo river, 95
Linyanti, 97–8
Livingstone, D., 99, 103, 118, 128–9, 140–1, 144, 146, 148; in South Africa, 96–9; Zambezi expedition, 100–1; in Central Africa, 131–2, 136–9; and *Last Journals*, 99; and *Missionary Travels*, 99; and *The Zambesi and its Tributaries*, 99, 101
Livingstone, Mary, 96, 99, 101
Loanda, 98
Lobo, J., 112; in East Africa, 19, 24, 29, 33, 39

INDEX

London Missionary Society, 96
Lualaba river, 131, 133, 137–8, 140–2, 144, 146, 149
Luama river, 144
Lucas, —, in North Africa, 42–3
Lukuga river, 140
Lyon, G., in North Africa, 57–9

Makololo, the, 97–100
Malawi, 101
Marinus of Tyre, 12–13
Masai, the, 113, 150
Massawa, 20, 24–6
Mecca, 14, 56, 110
Mediterranean, 9–11, 16, 57, 62, 149
Michael, Ras, 26–9, 33–4
Moffat, R., 96
Mombasa, 103–4, 106, 113
Monteil, P. L., in North Africa, 93
Moon, Mountains of the, 12–13, 62, 112, 117 and n, 150
Moors, the, 47–8, 73, 75
Morocco, 55, 75, 91
Mozambique, 107
Murchison Falls, 127
Murchison, Sir R., 99, 116, 127, 129, 131
Murzuk, 43, 57, 59–60, 84, 89
Mutesa, king of Buganda, 118–119, 143–4, 149
Mweru, Lake, 131, 133

Nachtigal, G., in North Africa, 92
Ngami, Lake, 97
Niger river, 11–14, 42–3, 45, 48, 50–3, 55–60, 62–5, 67–71, 73–74, 76–83, 86–7, 90–3, 118
Nile river, 9–12, 14, 20, 22, 24, 30, 33, 37–9, 42, 55, 59, 68, 70, 89, 94, 109–10, 121–2, 126–8, 130–1, 135, 137, 140, 146; search for sources of, 13, 112–13, 115–18, 119–123, 125–129, 131, 138–9, 141–3, 149, 150
Nile, the Blue, 12, 19–20, 24, 27, 30–33, 37, 39–40, 113
Norden, F., and the Nile, 20, 24
Nubian Desert, 56
Nun river, 80–1
Nyangwe, 138, 141, 144
Nyasa, Lake, 101, 118, 131, 150
Nyika, the, 103

Ogowe river, 149
Orange river, 21, 95
Oudney, W., 63–4, 84; in North Africa, 59–61
Overweg, L., in North Africa, 83–7

Paez, P., 112; in Ethiopia, 18–19, 24, 33, 39
Park, M., 55–9, 63–4, 69, 73–4, 82, 87–8, 90–1; in North and West Africa, 43–9, 50–4; and *Travels in the Interior Districts of Africa*, 49
Pascoe, 68–9, 71–2, 76, 78, 80, 82
Peddie, —, in North and West Africa, 56, 73
Pocock, E. and F., 142, 147–8
Pococke, R., 20, 24
Poncet, J. C., in Ethiopia, 19–20, 35
Prince Consort, 107, 123
Ptolemy, 12–13

Quilimane, 99–100

Rabai, 103, 105, 107, 109

Rebmann, J., 109, 113, 151; in East Africa, 103–8

Red Sea, coasts of, 10, 16, 19–20, 24–5, 56, 94, 112

Richardson, J., in North Africa, 83–5

Ripon Falls, 121, 142–3

Ritchie, J., in North Africa, 57–58

Rohlfs, G., 83; in North and West Africa, 91–2; in Ethiopia, 92

Rose, B., 66 n

Rovuma river, 131

Royal Geographical Society, 82, 89, 92–3, 99, 105, 112, 116–18, 121, 127, 131, 139, 141

Rukwa, Lake, 150

Rumanika, king of Karagwe, 118–19, 144

Rusizi river, 115, 128, 137, 142–143

Ruwenzori Mountains—see Mountains of the Moon

Sahara, 9, 13–14, 43, 83, 92

Schnitzer, E., in Central Africa, 140–1, 149–50

Schweinfurth, G., in North Africa; and *The Heart of Africa*, 130–1

Scott, Sir W., 49–50

Semliki river, 126, 141

Senegal, 43, 73–4, 93

Senegal river, 10, 17–18, 42, 52, 56, 73

Sennar, 20, 24, 35–7, 62

Shari river, 60–1, 63, 86

Shendy, 37, 56

Shire Highlands, 101, 131

Shirwa, Lake, 101

Shoa, the, 102

Sierra Leone, 11, 54, 58, 63, 66

Slave trade, 18, 46, 49, 57, 60, 67, 71, 84, 95, 98, 100–1, 121, 123, 130–1, 138–9, 141, 144; British abolition of, 41, 62, 95

Sokoto, 62–3, 65, 69, 87–8, 93

Somali, the, 110

Somali Republic, 94, 107, 110–111

Somerset Nile river, 126, 140

Speke, J. H., 127–131, 135, 137, 140, 142–3; in Ethiopia and the Somali Republic, 111; in East Africa, 112–123; and *Journal of the discovery of the source of the Nile*, 119

Stanley Falls, 146

Stanley, H. M., 117 n, 126, 129, 133–4, 138, 141, 150–1; in Central Africa, 135–7, 141–150; and *How I Found Livingstone*, 134–7, 141; and *Through the Dark Continent*, 144–5, 148–149

Stanley Pool, 147, 149

Sudan, 10, 12–14, 20, 58, 75, 121

Sudd, 12

Susi, 131, 138, 140

Tabora, 113–15, 118, 140

Tafilet, 91–2

Tana, Lake, 19–20, 26, 28, 30–1

Tana river, 107

Tanganyika, Lake, 105–6, 112, 114–15, 117–18, 128, 131, 133, 137, 140–2, 144, 150

Tangier, 14, 75, 91

Tanzania, 14, 105, 107, 113

Tecla Haimanot, 26–9

Thomson, J., in Central Africa, 150–1; and *Mungo Park and the Niger*, 91

Timba, Lake, 149
Timbuktu, 13–15, 42, 49, 57–9, 63–8, 73–5, 87–8, 90–2, 151
Tippu Tib, 144
Tisisat Falls, 19, 28–9
Tripoli, 57, 59, 62–4, 66, 70, 83–4, 89, 92–3
Tuareg tribe, 65–6, 69, 75, 84–5
Tuckey, J. H., on the Congo, 56

Ujiji, 114–15, 133, 136–8, 140–1, 144

Victoria Falls, 98–9
Victoria, Lake, 115–122, 126–9, 140–4, 149–50
Victoria, Queen, 126
Vogel, E., in North Africa, 88–9, 92

Volta river, 92

Wadai, 89, 92
Wady Sus, 91
Wainwright, J., 138
Wakamba, the, 106

Yasin, 25, 35
Yorubas, the, 65, 68, 76

Zambezi river, 97–101, 131
Zanzibar, 13, 92, 94, 101–3, 113, 122, 135, 138–9, 142, 148–50
Zaria, 69, 71
Zinder, 85
Zulus, the, 95